Around the Peat-fire

Around the Peat-fire

Calum Smith

BIRLINN

This edition first published in 2010 by
Birlinn Limited
West Newington House
10 Newington Road
Edinburgh
EH9 1QS

www.birlinn.co.uk

First published in 2001 by Birlinn Limited
Expanded edition, with Selected Journalism,
first published in 2010

ISBN 978 1 84158 904 6

British Library Cataloguing-in-Publication Data
A catalogue record for this book is available from the
British Library

Designed and typeset by Textype, Cambridge
Printed and bound by Cox & Wyman Ltd, Reading

For Marjory

Contents

Bith cianalas air Leodhasach ann a neamh
A Lewis person will be homesick in Heaven

Biographical Note

CALUM SMITH WAS born on 29 May 1912 in a *taigh-dubh* or thatched cottage, in Shawbost. He attended Shawbost and then Laxdale Primary schools, overcoming the difficulties of a native Gaelic speaker taught in an all-English medium. He was a secondary pupil in the Nicolson Institute, winning the competitive Bursary exam in his first year, playing for the first-eleven football team, becoming sports champion and taking the first ever gymnastics prize. He attended Glasgow University in the early thirties, where he studied English and Moral Philosophy with much enthusiasm and Latin with much less. He took part in boxing and athletics, and university politics as a member of the University Socialist Society. He left university in 1936 without a degree, a circumstance perhaps not unrelated to his involvement in extra-curricular activities.

Calum became a farm labourer at the Macaulay Demonstration Farm on the outskirts of Stornoway and then worked as a temporary clerk at the Stornoway

Labour Exchange, where he met his future wife, Peggy Flett. They were married in 1942.

During the Second World War Calum saw active service in the Royal Navy Patrol Service. He made numerous friends in the Navy but disliked many aspects of the war, and in particular the confines of the small boats in which he served; on his way home in 1945 he threw his naval uniform into the Minch.

After the war Calum worked for some time as an agent for an insurance company, but he proved to be something of a disappointment to his employers when he refused to sell inappropriate policies to poor Harris and Lewis householders, and it was with relief that he began work with the North of Scotland Hydro-Electric Board, initially as assistant cashier.

He was heavily involved in local politics, serving as chairman of the Western Isles Constituency Labour Party, championing the cause of the homeless and in particular the welfare of ex-servicemen. He served on the Stornoway Town council as Dean of Guild and Senior Baillie, and was a member of the Stornoway Trust. He worked tirelessly campaigning for the Labour Party in local and national elections, and was a frequent and powerful speaker at local political meetings.

He was an occasional contributor to the *Stornoway Gazette*, and it was when he lost his seat on the Council in 1955 that he was asked by the Gazette to contribute a regular column called 'As I See It', a reflective and often hard-hitting commentary on local and national affairs.

Calum loved walking – during their courtship he and Peggy spent much time walking all over Lewis. Calum did not drive and always said that he would rather polish his boots whilst others polished their cars. He had become a keen golfer since giving up football in the forties, and was a founder member of Stornoway Golf Club when it was resurrected after the Second World War. He won championships and trophies in Stornoway and later in Strathpeffer.

Due to reorganisation within the Hydro Board Calum and Peggy moved to Dingwall in 1959 with their family. Calum retired at the age of 65 and moved to Cullen on the Moray coast where he and Peggy enjoyed life to the full, keeping fit through walking. He played golf well into his eighties – 'Not too bad for an old man!' he would say with some satisfaction as his ball soared up the centre of the fairway into the middle distance and well beyond his own range of vision!

Calum's long retirement allowed him the time to write a book which was published in 2001, entitled *Around the Peat-fire*, a unique and fascinating account of Hebridean life in the first half of the last century. He derived much pleasure from Gaelic culture. His knowledge of literature – both Gaelic and English – was extensive, and he was able to quote long passages of poetry from memory and to offer an almost simultaneous English translation, often of great beauty in its own right, of Gaelic poetry and song. His interest in politics and his readiness for an argument never waned. He was a noted public speaker, and returned to Stornoway in 1974 to attend the 50th Anniversary dinner of the Stornoway Trust as one of the guests of honour to give the after dinner address, and again in 1975 to propose the toast to the Council's officers and staff at the Final Adjournment dinner of the Stornoway Town Council.

Calum died in November 2003 at the age of 91.

1

Survival

THE YEAR WAS 1912; the date the twenty-ninth day of
May. In a little geo at the village of Shawbost on the
Atlantic coast of Lewis in the Western Isles a group of
crofter women were gathering seaweed. The inward
surge of *an ataireachd bhuan* (the everlasting swell)
swirled up to their feet. Beneath the outward heave of the
receding water the shingle grumbled.

It was a situation where, even on a fine day, some
degree of watchfulness was necessary. The women knew
this from long experience and were taking due care as
they toiled. One of them, however, appeared to be more
cautious in her movements than the rest; and her older
sister, who was also in the group, quipped, 'You are
making sure that the *tonn bhaite* [drowning wave]
doesn't catch you today!' This was good-natured banter,
because the younger sister was in an obvious and very
advanced state of pregnancy; perhaps her extra
watchfulness was more for the burden that she was
carrying than for herself.

When the weed was gathered and the creels filled the

group climbed out of the geo and carried their slippery loads back to the village.

The pregnant woman was my mother, and I was born that evening. I know it was that same evening because I was told so; certainly the fact could not be established from my birth certificate, which states the time of birth as '8.26 a.m. p.m.' and the date as '39th [crossed out] 29th May 1912'.

My wife maintains that the registrar must have been drunk, but I am inclined to the opinion that it is just one more example of Gaelic thought being translated laboriously into English, the official language of registration.

Considered in the context of the stringent economic conditions obtaining in that society at that time, my being born at all was an unwarranted extravagance on the part of my parents; and considered in relation to the family infant mortality rate my birth was a flip in the face of fate.

My mother and father were twenty-eight years of age: of the three children, all boys, born to them before my appearance on that May evening, one was left. The other two had survived for only two or three weeks.

The high incidence of infant infection and death is not really surprising when one considers the living conditions of the time, and compares these conditions with modern concepts of health and hygiene.

The floors were of clay, the walls were of stone and earth, the roof was thatch with stalactites of peat-soot hanging from the rafters, there was no running water, no toilet facilities, the cattle were often under the same roof although in another part of the building, the hens were in and out pecking at anything that suggested sustenance, and fresh air inside the house was considered to be highly dangerous, especially for infants.

Furthermore the mother was virtually starved for a week or ten days after confinement. For that period the staple diet was tea and toast, and the idea of giving her a full and sustaining meal was considered as putting her life at risk. Consequently the new-born breast-fed child must have been doing rather badly on milk from a hungry and ill-nourished mother.

Within a very few days after entering this inhospitable environment I, also, became a victim of one or more of the numerous bugs that were lying in wait for the weak; and it soon became quite apparent to all concerned, including the family doctor, that for me the passage from 'Entrance' to 'Exit' was going to be very short indeed. The doctor told my parents that he thought they should arrange to have me baptised as soon as possible – perhaps a considerate way of conveying to them the grim truth that I was about to die.

The harsh brand of Presbyterianism holding sway at the time saw nothing incongruous in the belief that a fatherly and loving God should condemn a newly born child to everlasting hellfire because he had not been subjected to the ritual of baptism.

So the minister came as soon as he was called, for this, although no longer a matter of life and death, was apparently very much a matter of life after death. The minister asked my father what the name was to be, and my father turned to my mother and said, 'What name do you wish to give him?' She replied: 'The two that we lost were both named Calum, and as we are losing this one I wish to name him Calum also.'

In a short Gaelic service I was therefore christened Calum.

When, some time later, having opted for the here and now rather than a hypothetical hereafter, the birth had to be registered. It was of course registered in English as Malcolm. This was the case with almost all Lewis children, apart from a few in the town of Stornoway; their christened or Christian names were Gaelic while their registered or birth certificate names were English.

Having survived this initial brush with fate I appear to have made a rapid recovery and to have gone on 'from strength to strength', manifested in an inordinate and sometimes boisterous vitality.

In later years my mother assured me that while still at the crawling stage, before I started walking, I developed to an almost obsessive degree a disposition towards climbing anything that was climbable, and many things that were not, with the inevitable consequences of repeated falls; and a mother who was in an almost perpetual state of nervous tension at the prospect of my braining myself as soon as her back was turned – and her back had to be turned often, because of the many things to which she must attend.

Her eternal cry, as I progressed from one outrage to the next was 'Oh, a dheamhain!' – 'Oh, you demon!' And both my mother and father have told me that the first word that they understood me to speak was *dheamhain*.

There is a Gaelic saying in Lewis, '*Is buan gach dheamhain*' – demons are durable. Could be one reason why I have survived so long.

But before being old enough to go to school I still had a few health hurdles to clear, and the only reason I mention these is that they illustrate that however sickly a child may be he can develop into a robust and quite active adult; and also because in two instances old wives' cures were applied.

At the age of three I developed a severe case of pneumonia in both lungs, and although I remember nothing of the illness I do recollect convalescing. In fact in my mind's eye I can still see the design of the coverlet on the box bed where I sat up supported by pillows, the shelved wooden box with odds and ends in it that lay across the foot of the bed so that I could play at shopkeeping; and especially I can remember the taste of the warm diluted milk and water that I was given to drink. Then, much later in convalescence, I remember the 'chemical food' that I was given in teaspoon doses several times a day.

Having recovered from that bout I was next assailed by a virulent jaundice, which resulted quite simply from a remark that was passed by my older brother while I was eating a boiled egg for breakfast, causing such extreme nausea that very shortly my skin became yellow in colour, while my squeamish stomach refused to retain any food that had not already been rejected by my looking at it and refusing to eat it.

The doctor was called in and apparently there was nothing very much that he could do. The facilities available in that locality more than eighty years ago must have been primitive indeed. So, as time passed and I wasted away from malnutrition, my mother was advised that she would just have to watch the process of my elimination by slow starvation.

It was at this stage that she decided to try an 'old wife's cure' that she had heard of as being effective; and it is a cure that I have cause to remember vividly.

Getting up one morning, instead of dressing as usual I was persuaded to sit on a stool in my nightdress in front of a blazing peat-fire while my mother got a clean shirt for me to wear. As I sat glowing in the relaxing peat warmth I was asked to take off my nightdress, which I did in the time-honoured way of clutching it from behind and pulling it forward over my head. It was then that I got a pail full of ice-cold water between the shoulder blades, and, as I turned round screaming, a large jug full of the same cold water hit me in the chest.

I can still see my mother with the jug in her hand in tears at what she was doing to me; but once I had been dried, warmed and dressed I was soon consoled. From that morning I began to recover. My appetite and colour came back, and very soon I was once again qualifying for the title of *deamhan*.

When considering this incident many years later I came to the conclusion that there was probably a sound medical basis of shock-therapy for what was generally considered to be a superstitious cure. What I do know is that a nauseating shock gave me what turned out to be almost lethal jaundice, and that a physical shock cured me.

The next thing to hit me was an infected gland on the left side of my neck which defied all the local doctor's efforts to deal with it, and just refused to heal. The general diagnosis among the village women was that my ailment was an obvious case of 'the King's Evil' (scrofula), for which numerous superstitious cures were available. As a last resort, when medical efforts had failed, a seventh son of a seventh son – fortuitously available in the village – was called in to assist: water in which he had dipped his fingers (what price modern hygiene?) was applied to the affected part, and a silver sixpence (he himself got another silver sixpence as his fee) in which he had made a hole with the aid of a sharp-pointed nail and a hammer, was hung round my neck on a cord. And, strange to tell, the suppurating gland began to show immediate signs of improvement and healed beautifully with none other than the water treatment.

I have tried, with hindsight, to think up a rational or medically credible explanation for this happening, but have been unable to come up with anything. It could not have been faith healing on my part, because I had no very clear idea of what was going on; nor on the part of my mother, because, as she told me later, she didn't believe that it would work, although she was prepared to try anything. Perhaps the infection had reached the stage where it would have healed anyway, even if left severely alone.

The environment into which I slipped on that twenty-ninth day of May was primitive in the extreme. The majority of the people of rural Lewis before the First World War lived in thatched cottages, many of them so constructed that separate accommodation was provided in the one building, under one roof, for humans and cattle.

My recollection of our house in Shawbost is that when you went in the front door the 'byre' and cattle were there immediately on the left, and on the right was a wall separating the dwelling house from the byre, and between them was a 'throughway' leading to the barn; the barn being a separate building, having a common wall with the main dwelling, and separately thatched.

On going in the front door, immediately on the right, in the wall, was a door giving access to the family quarters; and in the middle of the wall was, on the family side, a fireplace and chimney. Then there was another wall, against which there was a box bed – it was in this bed that I lay recovering from double pneumonia when I was three years old – and to the right of the bed was a door leading to the sleeping accommodation, where, if my memory serves me, there were two beds.

In the main room, in addition to the box bed, there was the 'dresser' with its crockery, the 'being' or bench, and the usual supply of all kitchen equipment (pots and pans etc.), together with a ready-to-use peat supply.

All the cooking was done on the open peat-fire in the chimney wall, as was all the baking. While on the cooking side the variety of dishes could be somewhat restricted because of limited facilities, on the baking side the *greideal* was a most adequate medium. All the bread was home baked (a baker's loaf was a rare luxury) and the scones and bannocks produced could be of flour, oatmeal, flour and oatmeal mixed, and barley.

All the water used for cooking, baking and washing (both of humans and clothes) was taken in pails from the nearest well. Sometimes, in a dry summer, the nearest well ran dry, and you had to go quite a distance to get a supply. Water is heavy to carry, and you had to go carefully to prevent too much loss by spillage. This was very frustrating, and especially so at weekends, because of the primitive attitude to Sabbath observance. In no circumstances must you go to the well for water on the Sabbath day, so all the water for weekend use had to be collected on Saturday and stored in pails and tubs for use until Monday morning. The provision of water on a Sunday, in dry, hot weather when water is scarce, would seem to many people to be a work of necessity and mercy, but the categorical imperative of the commandment is thou shalt not do *any* work! 'Necessity and mercy' are not mentioned in the Bible.

Another primitive restraint that operated was that all requirements for Sunday cooking had to be prepared on Saturday evening – potatoes peeled, cabbage washed, turnips peeled and chopped, carrots scraped and so on.

There is quite a good story, arising from the Saturday

vegetable preparation, that I must include here. A young man from Glasgow married a Hebridean girl who belonged to a very strict Free Presbyterian household, and the first summer after they were married they decided to go to her parents' home for the summer holiday. One of the first things sorted out was, of course, the churchgoing arrangements. These were that the parents and young folk would go on alternate Sundays, the ones staying at home preparing the Sunday dinner; and it was agreed that the father and mother should go the first Sunday.

So they did, and when they got home the table was beautifully set and everything laid on for dinner. On sitting down the father said the usual elaborate Presbyterian grace, and the soup was dished. The soup is always dished after the grace in these households, because the grace is usually so long that the soup would be cold if it were dished first.

After they had got further on in the meal the son-in-law noticed that his father-in-law was not eating any potatoes, and said: 'I see you are not eating any potatoes. Do you not like the way they are cooked?'

'It is not that,' said the old man. 'These potatoes were peeled on Sunday. That is a sin. So I cannot eat them.'

The following Sunday it was the turn of the young couple to go to church. And when they sat down to dinner afterwards the only difference from the previous Sunday appeared to be that the potatoes were not peeled.

This time it was the young man who was not eating potatoes; and his father-in-law said, 'I see you are not eating the potatoes. Do you not like potatoes in their jackets?'

'Oh, I like them fine,' he said. 'It's not that. It is that you told me that it is a sin to peel potatoes on a Sunday. And

I cannot eat them with the peels on.' A reply which must have given his host food for thought!

Another restricting aspect of this environment was the superstition that was prevalent and systematically fostered by dedicated *seanachies* – storytellers.

I, like all my fellows, was subjected during what were very important years in my development to every superstitious influence calculated to make an abject and drivelling coward of me for the rest of my days.

Every *cailleach* and *bodach* (old woman and old man) in the neighbourhood took a ghoulish delight in filling my youthful mind with the dire terrors of ghosts, hauntings, second sight, and all that was eerie and uncanny in their own minds. Even the simplest occurrences were sometimes vested with a dark dread.

The roll of thunder, the flash of lightning, the crowing of the barnyard cockerel at an unusual hour, the baying of the domestic dog at the moon, the ticking of the death-watch beetle, were all divested of their natural and commonplace significance and imbued with fearful meanings which had their source in ignorance and a darkness of the mind.

Generation after generation gathered round peat-fires on dark winter nights, while the storytellers vied with one another to make each tale more hair-raising than the last.

In addition to the *cailleachs* and *bodachs*, however, there were also the occasional non-conformists, who told tales of ghosts that weren't, ghosts that were created to frighten the superstitious believers. And with some of these I shall be dealing later on.

In addition to the primitive conditions, both physical and intellectual, that obtained, another factor that must be considered is the harsh stringency of economic conditions at that time; economic conditions that were the main cause of the primitive conditions.

The general terrain in Lewis, from an agricultural point of view, is as unproductive as can be found anywhere in Scotland, and the process of producing crops, where this is possible, entails backbreaking physical effort. It was only in limited areas that a plough could be used for digging or drilling. Consequently most of that kind of work was done with the spade, the hoe, the *graip* (fork) and the *croman*. The *croman* was an all-purpose implement with a curved, narrow, heavy, pointed blade and had a shaft much shorter and heavier than a hoe. It had many uses where a deal of the work had to be done on sparse rocky soil.

Incidentally a friend of mine, who had been brought up on a croft, but who had attained the social status of being a golfer, always referred to his pitching wedge as a 'croman'.

On that soil the standard crops were potatoes, oats and barley. The potato was the main crop, as it was in Ireland; the staple diet of the population. The oats and barley were dried in a peat-heated little local kiln and ground into meal in the local mill. I remember being with my mother and father, shortly after the First World War (I would have been seven or eight years old at the time) in the kiln in Shawbost drying barley, and being at the water-operated mill when it was being ground down into meal.

I personally did not find barley bread as palatable as oat or flour bread. But it was very sustaining, and many years after partaking of this product of our own little croft I remember an old retired Lewis fisherman, apropos of something that we were discussing saying, 'Cha do dh-ith me biadh a riabh a b'aide chumadh mo cridhe rium na sgadan sailt 's aran eorna' – 'I never ate food that would keep heart in me longer than salt herrings and barley bread.'

In the spring when the winter stored food was dwindling the cured dog-fish (*bireach*) were brought to the fore. In the Atlantic, from villages on the west coast, the *bireach* was very extensively fished. The fish were split, cleaned and heavily salted. Then they were set out to dry and harden on any drystone dykes available, and when they were considered to be fully cured they were stored for future use. Those retained for ready use were hung on a line (*sioman*) across the living-room, under the roof. Here, from the peatsmoke, they developed a pleasing smoky flavour, and if you wanted a quick snack to have with a potato, a piece of this smoky *bireach* was placed across the end of the tongs and held over the glowing embers of the peat-fire. Any additional peat smoke only improved the flavour. I myself have seen this done many times.

In addition to the salting of fish of different kinds, meat was also preserved in the same way. But before this method of preservation was introduced, the practice, common in Lewis, was to bury the carcass of the slaughtered animal in peat. A great pit was dug in a place where the peat was very deep; the animal being preserved was then slaughtered and tipped into this pit. When dug up in the spring it was perfect, and most welcome, for immediate consumption. The meat preserved in this way was referred to as *feoil reisg* – peat meat. When the method of salting and combined salting and smoking had taken over, the newly developed product was referred to as *feoil reisg*; the title 'peat meat' had been adopted and accepted as the proper description for preserved meat. I myself remember eating salt mutton that was called '*feoil reisg*', but it very definitely was not peat meat.

By the way, if my memory can be trusted (it was a long time ago) the very best soup or broth ever made was based on Lewis-cured salt mutton.

These methods of fish and meat preservation, that were so vital a part of that stringent economy, have now been ousted by the deep freeze. And the deep freeze was taken up so enthusiastically by the Islesmen that a commercial representative of the northern area of the North of Scotland Hydroelectric remarked to me (knowing that I was a Lewisman), 'The crofters of Lewis pioneered the use of the deep freeze in the Highlands of Scotland.'

To cope with economic circumstances in this deprived environment the policy adopted was, to my mind, that of a practical form of communism. The whole survival system was based on mutual and neighbourly helpfulness and cooperation. All that had to be done was done by groups working together. Croft work, peat cutting, drying of peats, creeling or barrowing to roadside, thatching of cottages, seagoing fishing, in fact anything that entailed work was done on this basis. And the orphans, the widows, the old, the disabled were all treated as members of their local working group, and everything that needed doing was done for them. At the same time there was no room for anyone that might try to take advantage of the system. The remedy was obvious – if you didn't pull your weight you did what had to be done for yourself, by yourself.

2

Beginning

UNTIL I WAS ABOUT seven years old, my father was away in the First World War as a Royal Naval Reservist. He had joined at the age of sixteen, as soon as he was big enough – this was the only qualification for a person medically fit – giving his age as eighteen. Forty-seven years later, because all the Ministry of Health and Ministry of Labour records showed his age as sixty-five, he had to produce a copy of his birth certificate to avoid being retired on an old-age pension at sixty-three.

Because he was away my upbringing in the early years was in the hands of my mother, and was conducted on a broad religious basis. The Lord's Prayer and the twenty-third psalm were learned by rote before I ever went to school; Gaelic psalms and hymns were sung to me as lullabies; I was told religious stories, including *The Pilgrim's Progress*, and also the occasional legendary Gaelic fairytale, often with superstitious undertones; and God was used as a correcting influence in lieu of an absent father.

When my father did come home I discovered that he was not a bit like God, of whom I was terrified, but was instead bubbling over with laughter and jokes, songs, poems and stories. However, it was some time yet before he was due to be demobilised.

Living in the family home were my grandmother and grandfather, my mother's mother and father, and before I was five years old my grandfather died.

My maternal grandparents were typical hard-working crofters. They dug the ground with spades. They carried what had to be carried on their backs in creels. But they also had some skills – my grandmother could do all that was required for the production of yarn from the local wool: washing, carding, dyeing and spinning, while my grandfather could weave the cloth on a wooden loom that he had in the barn. He could also make creels from willows grown in little walled gardens on the croft.

The morning that my grandfather died I noticed at breakfast time that my older brother John was looking upset and didn't appear to be interested in his breakfast. Of course I wanted to know what was wrong, but I was fobbed off with some explanation that satisfied me at the time. One of the tricks of my memory is that I recollect quite clearly asking John why he had been crying and wasn't interested in his food. I remember my mother intervening with an explanation; but I do not recall what she actually said.

After breakfast I got on with my own affairs as usual, with no knowledge of the bereavement that had struck, nor was there a gentle breaking of the news when it did come.

The play that morning was boats, and a block of wood, roughly shaped with a stem and stern, and with two sticks set in holes fore and aft for masts, was launched on a roadside pool not far from the house. There I was, full of infant glee, pushing the boat out to sea across the pond, then dashing round to retrieve it and push it back again, when I became aware of a presence watching me. Looking up I saw a man there, standing over me, clad from head to foot in sombre black, his grey face lined and grim; in a grey, grim, religious voice he asked me: 'What are you doing, playing there, when your grandfather is dead?'

Many years later when I thought back on that short sharp shock I regretted that I didn't believe in hell, because if I did there would be a special place in it for people like that.

The toy boat and my seafaring adventure were abandoned as I went dashing home, where it was immediately obvious to my mother that I knew the truth. I didn't cry, possibly I was too shocked; and also I probably felt guilty because I had been playing. But the day of the funeral brought relief.

I sat silent and still, gazing at the polished brown coffin, while the women sobbed, the whole gathering wailed a Gaelic psalm, and the church elders chanted their prayers. Then, as soon as the service was over, I was overwhelmed by an abrupt realisation that inside that polished brown box was my grandfather, that it would be carried out of the house, and that I would never see him again. As I sobbed silently and the tears ran down my face my mother found time, even at that grief-drenched moment, for it was her father that was dead, to come over to me and put her arm round my shoulders. The passing of time did the rest.

Shortly after this another brother appeared on the scene and he was given my grandfather's name, Angus. There were now four children. A sister Mary had been born in 1914 before my father went away to the war.

That same year that grandfather died and Angus was born I went to school for the first time and I fear that my initial reaction to the experience stayed with me all my life.

Sitting still and remaining silent were requirements for which I was in no way qualified, and that very first morning I found the situation so intolerably boring that I just got out of my seat, made my way down the passage between the rows, crossed the classroom floor, opened the door and walked out. It says a great deal for the infant mistress that she paid, or appeared to pay, no attention at all to what was going on.

However, having walked out I soon discovered that the boredom of being the solitary occupant of a large playground far exceeded that of being a member of a large class, and after the morning interval I returned with the other pupils – again apparently unnoticed. The only time I ever left my class after that during school hours was when I was thrown out.

With English primers and English arithmetic books, teaching reading and counting to a Gaelic-speaking class of five-year-olds – none of whom spoke a word of English – must have been quite a task for infant-school mistresses in the Hebrides. Gaelic was used as a vehicle for communication, and after a period of chanting 'C-A-T: cat, M-A-T: mat, R-A-T: rat' or 'one and one two, two and two four' we would be questioned 'A nis, de th'ann C-A-T?' or 'A nis de th'ann one and one?' – 'Now, what is C-A-T?' or 'Now, what is one and one?'

In the beginning progress must have been understandably slow, and it was certainly slow for me, as I overheard my teacher having a quiet word with my mother because of my lack of progress. I had a dreadful lisp and a hesitancy that was almost a stammer. It wasn't that I didn't know how to read, but that I couldn't get the words out, and when I did my lisp made things additionally difficult.

Although I started to speak early, beginning as I explained with the word *deamhan*, and have been speaking almost non-stop ever since, the quality if not the quantity of the speech was suspect. My mother had even had the doctor examine my tongue to see whether there was any physical explanation for my handicap. He assured her that he could find no reason for my condition; and although the hesitancy disappeared quite early the lisp stayed with me until I was well into my teens. Of course many of my classmates thought it was great fun to mock me by repeating, with due exaggeration, some of my more obvious lisping lapses. This could be one of the reasons why a therapeutic amnesia prevents me remembering very much of what happened in the four years that I spent at Shawbost school.

There were no school uniforms in the villages of Lewis in those days; the children's underwear was usually run up by the mothers from any suitable cloth that was available; in fact in some instances the cloth used for making a boy's shirt was a carefully washed flour bag. The outer garments were usually a woollen jersey, a pair of short trousers – very often readjusted cast-offs – woollen stockings and steel-plated and heeled tackety boots.

The only game that I remember playing during school intervals or playtime was a primitive form of shinty which we called *gioman*. The *camans* or sticks were home-made and were as varied in appearance and usefulness as were the personalities of those who had produced them. The ball was also home-made and was often nothing more elaborate than the cork from a herring net. The rules were flexible, as was the manner (often highly dangerous because of boisterous boyish exuberance) in which the *camans* were wielded. Eighty years later I still carry a small scar on the third finger of my right hand where it got in the way of one of those swings.

We usually played on the road or in a very small field below the school, and when the headmaster's whistle signalled the end of playtime the shinty sticks were flung in a shower over the nearest fence to be scrambled for and retrieved when next we got out for play.

In that village, however, life outside the school was really something to be savoured, especially during the long summer holidays, and how beautifully long the holidays seem when one is young.

With the first sunny day of spring the pleading started to be allowed to discard the 'tackety boots' that had been worn all winter, and to go barefoot until the end of autumn. There is nothing quite like the buoyancy of that airborne feeling on the first barefoot day in spring. I virtually took off, bounding as if I had suddenly sprouted wings. There was so much to do – the river, the sandy fringe of Loch a Bhaile, the beach, the rock pools, the geos, the crofts, the peats, the moors – all were there; and although the summer days were long they were never long enough.

There are some things that I remember with particular pleasure: walking barefoot in lush wet grass on a sunny morning after a shower of rain and smelling the wild hyacinths; the smell and taste of wild honey from the hives that we found and raided; the tang of the sea mingled with that of sun-drenched seaweed and tarry rope; the whiff of dry heather burning as kindling for a peat-fire; the pungency of peat smoke. What a place that was in which to be young!

3

The *Iolaire*

Without doubt the greatest influence in my young life was the return of my father from the war when I was seven years old: my first memory of him is that of himself and his brother John standing in our house in naval uniform waiting to go back from leave, and Uncle John quietly smiling as he made some derisive comment about my father giving my mother a farewell peck. I never saw uncle John again, for he was drowned in the *Iolaire* disaster of 1 January 1919. This tragedy, in which 181 island seamen died on their own doorstep after surviving the war, has been talked and written about for over sixty years; I remember it as a six-and-a-half-year-old who watched the horses and carts with their burdens of coffins going head to tail along the main road to the Bragar cemetery. The *Iolaire* went down because she missed the entrance to Stornoway harbour and foundered on the rocks known as the Beasts of Holm. A full account of the disaster is contained in a book entitled *Sea Sorrow* published by the *Stornoway Gazette* in 1972.

This gives a detailed account of the enquiry into the disaster, the findings of the jury and lists of casulaties.

Before the news that day in 1919 broke a group of us were standing in front of one of the croft houses in North Shawbost when a sailor in uniform came trudging wearily along the street with his head down. We recognised him, and as he went past one of the boys called, 'A Mhurchaidh, an ainig m'athair 'sa raoir?' – 'Murdo, did my father come last night?' We all thought it strange that Murdo didn't lift his downcast head, look round or make any response. Later that day we heard what had happened and that Murdo was one of the survivors, and we understood.

When the news did come through my recollection is of everything suddenly going very quiet, of women talking in hushed voices: it was as if there was a feeling that noise would be an offence to the dead.

Then I heard my mother telling my older brother that Uncle John had been expected home and was not known to be among the survivors. As he and my father had gone away together after their last leave she thought it possible that my father might have been on board too, although she did not have the customary warning telegram; she had wired to him at HMS *Ganges* and had received a reassuring reply.

One of my most vivid recollections is of sitting in a neighbouring house the following day as one of the survivors sat on a stool in front of a large peat-fire, with his trousers legs rolled up, while his mother knelt at his feet, bathing them in warm water, drying them very gently with a heated towel, and then smearing Vaseline on the cuts and abrasions that he had sustained clambering up the rocks at Holm in his socks.

It was a time of desolation, and of a grief that still,

after more than eighty years, touches those who remember.

Thirty-five years after the disaster I gained an insight into it from an angle not touched upon before. There was stationed in Stornoway at the time a Lieutenant Townend RNR, who did compass adjustments for trawlers and other small vessels using the port. It was after he had retired as Captain Townend, principal of the Nautical College in Grimsby, that I met him. He had been wakened in the middle of the night by the landlord of his billet on Church Street shaking him and muttering something like 'Why are you sleeping warmly there when Lewis seamen are drowning on the Beasts of Holm?' 'Talking almost as if it were my fault,' said Captain Townend.

When told what had happened he got up at once, dressed quickly, and went down to the base. There follows a paraphrase, from memory, of what he said to me:

In the morning the base Commander ordered me to take charge of all the bodies brought in, pending identification and awaiting collection for burial. It was a situation on which there was nothing in the Manual of Seamanship, and with which I simply did not know how to cope.

So I approached the Master-at-Arms, told him what I had to do, and said, 'Forget that I am an officer, and from your long service and experience, tell me as man to man, how would you go about this?'

The Master-at-Arms came to attention, saluted and said: 'Whatever you say, sir.'

I said, 'Never mind saluting and being "purser",

as man to man, what do I do?'

Again he saluted and said, 'Whatever you say, sir.'

I hesitated for a moment, and then I came to attention and rapped out, 'Clear the ammunition store!'

'But sir . . .' He got no further as I snapped 'Clear the ammunition store! THAT is an ORDER!'

While the store was being cleared I was thinking things out.

I requisitioned a supply of strong, brown paper bags from the Naafi, and as the bodies were brought in and laid out on the floor of the ammunition store, the contents of the pockets, cap tallies, anything that might help with identification, were put into one of the bags, the bag was numbered, and the same number was chalked on the boot-soles of the body – most of them were wearing their boots – or on a tag attached to the clothing.

Watching the relatives of missing men searching for their dead was the most harrowing experience of my life; especially when an identification was made. For months after it was all over I saw in my dreams rows of naval issue boots with numbers chalked on their soles.

4

Armistice

THIS DIGRESSION ON THE *Iolaire* disaster began by my talking of my father and uncle being home on leave together, and surprisingly for such a young child I recall a number of things that happened during the First World War.

There was, for instance, a soldier in khaki who made his way down to the shore, and looking out over the Atlantic fired shot after shot from his rifle. I was on the *fadhlainn* between Loch a Bhaile and the sea at the time and couldn't see or understand what he was firing at. When I spoke about it after I got home I was told that it was the last evening of his leave and that he was setting off for France the following day – but I still didn't understand why he stood on the beach shooting out to sea.

One of my clearest recollections is of the funeral of a soldier who had died at home of a gangrenous wound sustained in the foul mud of Flanders.

The procession was of black-clad non-combatants,

almost entirely old men who were left at home – with one exception. Almost in the middle of the average-height black column there loomed a khaki-clad head and shoulders. It was Alec 'an Alasdair, that giant of a man from the Pairc, who was home on leave at the time. His presence there is very likely the reason for the picture remaining so clearly in my mind.

I have a very good reason for remembering another soldier being on leave. One morning I went with my mother to the local shop. I was barefoot: we were standing at the back waiting to be served, when the soldier, who was standing near the counter also waiting, stepped back and put the heel of his army boot on the toes of my left foot, and kept it there.

He was quite unaware of what he was doing, possibly because of the uneven floor, and I was much too shy to tell him. Nor did my mother, who was holding my hand, notice anything amiss, until, after he had moved to the counter, she saw me rubbing the bloody toes of the injured foot against the calf of the other leg. She was horrified when she saw my foot, but I didn't tell her what had happened until the soldier was safely out of the shop.

Then there was that wonderful day when news came of the Armistice – the feeling of release was passed on to the young by the grown-ups, and boys struggled to housetops to hoist white flags for peace on anything that might serve as a flagpole; even bamboo fishing rods were used.

One factor that contributed significantly to the island economy was the 'retainer' paid to the Royal Naval Reservists, of whom there were many thousands in Lewis. This meant that actual ready money went into circulation. And very welcome it was, especially for payment of rent, which had ever been a difficulty with crofters: they were able to live off the crofts and the surrounding sea but actual cash was scarce indeed. When my own grandmother was twelve years old her family was evicted from their croft in Valtos Uig, in the middle of the nineteenth century, because of rent arrears.

Many of the reservists were also merchant seamen; and most of them, when they got their pay, were mindful of the families they had left at home. This also was an important factor in putting cash into circulation.

The Royal Naval Reserve (RNR) was joined and accepted as an economic necessity. In some households a father and son, or sons, would have joined; or two or three brothers. In my own father's family my father and uncles Norman, Findlay and John were RNR. The four of them went off in August 1914, when I was two years old, and served throughout the First World War.

For a long time the Lewisman has had a great reputation as a seaman, and I experienced a patent example of this while serving myself, many years later, in the Second World War.

I was drafted to a ship that was engaged in convoy work in E-boat alley. Going down the gangway a lieutenant (two ringer) RNR was waiting. I set down my kitbag and my case, came to attention, saluted and reported, 'Able Seaman Malcolm Smith reporting for duty, sir.'

My accent had given me away; the greeting I got from the First Lieutenant was, 'You're a Stornoway man!'

'Yes, sir.'

'Right Mac! Put your gear in the foc'sle mess, report back, and I will give you your watch and duties.'

Although I had introduced myself as Smith, being a

27

'Stornoway man' I immediately became 'Mac' and remained 'Mac' all the time I served on that ship. I got rid of my kitbag and case and reported back to the First Lieutenant to be greeted as before: 'Right, Mac. Starboard Watch: Harbour station – Foc's'le mooring party; Seagoing station – Quartermaster; Action station – Breech worker on the four-inch gun; Abandon ship station – Stroke paddle in the port Carley Float.'

He didn't ask me whether I had ever moored a ship, steered a ship, been on a gun, or used a paddle in a Carley Float. I was a 'Stornoway man' – a Lewis able seaman. I was accepted without question, not for myself, but because of the reputation of Lewismen as seamen.

5

Father

WHEN MY FATHER DID come home at last, I think it
was in May 1919, a new dimension entered my
life. He seemed to be laughing all the time, and his blue
eyes sparkled as he went his extrovert way about whatever
he was doing. And there was always plenty to do. During
the war years my mother had kept the croft going, assisted
by what casual labour she could muster, which, if I
remember, consisted of teenagers under military age.

Now that my father was home, he took over, and
introduced a new and revolutionary method of working.
Behind our house was a hill, Cnoc Shithealair, which
descended steeply to a stretch of level ground bordering
Loch a Bhaile and the right banks of the Shawbost river.
All materials going into this lower stretch of croft –
manure, seed potatoes, oats and barley – and the
resulting crops coming out, had to be transported in
creels: it was backbreaking work, and climbing the hill
with the empty creels was almost as tiring as the cautious
descent with full loads.

Having decided that this work should be done henceforth by horse and cart my father spent many hours with spade and pick shifting great mounds of obstructive terrain, until he had achieved what he thought was a passable track, even if nothing remotely like what could be called a road.

This done he hitched our horse, Simmie Ruadh (Red Jimmy), into the cart and set off with a test load. But he had been over-optimistic, and on a two-way pitch on the left shoulder of the hill the cart capsised, taking Simmie with it.

I was there following the cart, and my father sprang to the horse's head holding it to the ground and preventing it struggling, and so averting a possible disaster. Soon neighbours were helping to unhitch the cart. Red Jimmy clambered to his feet none the worse for the mishap; and, miraculously, the cart had sustained negligible damage.

Quite undiscouraged by this mishap, and having made minor adjustments to the track with some more explosive use of the spade, my father had another go, this time taking the full load all the way down. His equine partner in this escapade had the heart of a lion and the agility of a steeplechaser; our Red Jimmy was as outstanding in his own class as was Red Rum in his, more than half a century later.

My Great-uncle Calum, whose croft was separated from ours by my cousin Colin's, was so astonished when he walked down his own croft and saw what had happened that he went back home and said to his wife Ceninag:

'Chunna mise rud an drasda nach fhaca duine riaimh ronna seo.'
'Ach de chunna du?'

'Chunna mi each is cart air rinn an ois'.'

'I have seen something just now that no-one has ever seen before.'
'But what did you see?'
'I saw a horse and cart at the river mouth!'

Needless to say working the lower part of the croft was a very much easier proposition from then on; and a particular bonus, I understood, was the fact that it was no longer necessary to carry seeping creels of manure on your back as part of the spring work.

In my young days, the recognised mode of transport was tackety boots or, on the moors, bare feet. The religious walked umpteen miles from district to district to attend communion. Working men sometimes walked seven or eight miles to work in the morning, and the same back in the evening after the work was done.

All journeys by ordinary working people were made on foot – fisher girls, herring gutters, fishermen, crofters, working men and women. Consequently, many tales of village activities included mention of the walking done.

My village was eighteen miles from Stornoway, and when my father came back from the war and he started carting to Stornoway, often with a load both ways. I remember hearing him say, 'I never sit in the cart if the horse is carrying a load.' Eighteen miles each way means, of course, that, one day's walking equals thirty-six miles.

It was only in later years that I realised the walking involved in some of the tales that I heard as a boy in my native village.

I remember hearing my grandmother telling of how she set off once to go shopping to Stornoway with the creel on her back – the recognised way to carry goods in those days. She was taking the route across the moors, somewhat shorter than the eighteen miles by road. On the way she passed a shieling, at the door of which a man was standing. After having a few words she told him she was going to Stornoway to do some shopping.

On the way back she met the same man again, and he greeted her with the question: 'Why did you turn back? You couldn't possibly have been to Stornoway since you passed here.'

'Oh but I was,' she said. 'And my purchases are in my creel!' She must have been an unusually fast walker.

It would have been in the second half of the nineteenth century, when distilling illicit whisky was a recognised leisure activity among the crofters of the Highlands and Islands, that one of our village women decided to cash in on this way of getting some extra money. She made the whisky and put it in two large stone jars, and put the jars in a creel. Then she asked a neighbour, who was known to be engaged in this activity, where in Stornoway she should go to sell the whisky.

Having got an address she set off for Stornoway with the creel on her back – eighteen miles by road, and nearly as far across the moors.

When she got there she went to the address she had been given and told the man who opened the door to her knock, 'A friend of mine gave me this address and said that you would buy the whisky that I made and have in my creel.'

'Well,' said the man, 'the person who gave you this address is no friend of yours. I am the exciseman. But as you obviously haven't done this before, I'll tell you what I'll do. If you give an undertaking that you will never distil whisky again, I will not prosecute, and I will give you an address where you can sell your whisky.'

Having given the undertaking she got the address, sold the whisky, and set off back home with the empty jars in her creel.

Crossing the Bragar River, two miles from home, she decided to have a drink, and let some of the river water trickle into one of the jars. She gave the jar a good shake, and poured the water into the other jar, shook that one up too, and had her drink.

The story goes that as she went into her village street she was showing a marked degree of unsteadiness! Not surprising, even without the whisky, after walking to Stornoway and back carrying her creel.

Mentioning Cnoc Shithealair, the hill behind our house, reminds me that it was from this eminence that my grandfather, Angus Macleod, was wont to blow trumpet blasts on the great conch shell (*conocag*), to alert the villagers that it was time to down their crofting implements and prepare for whatever the particular occasion might demand.

Although he died before I was five years old I have a clear recollection, in one instance, of being at the river end of the croft and seeing him standing on the hill, holding the shell to his lips, while what were, for me, quite awesome sounds reverberated towards the far horizons.

I remember seeing the *conocag* in the house, but only on the one occasion do I remember seeing and hearing it in use, and a vague something very far back tells me it was for a funeral. I often wondered in later years what happened to that conch shell.

My father had a repertoire of engaging stories, poems, and songs which I was only too ready to tap with whatever cajolery I could muster.

Ever since my bout of jaundice I was inclined to be a

trifle fastidious about some aspects of diet, and I soon discovered that one thing my father set great store by was that we should be well fed. All I had to say at supper time was, 'I can't eat my porridge' for him to sit astride the long stool, opposite me, regaling me with tales and rhymes, while I devoured his words and my supper in wide-eyed and wide-mouthed absorption. The recital stopped when the plate and milk-bowl were empty. But we both knew it was a game.

I discovered many years later that he knew all Neil Macleod's stories in *Clarsach an Doire* almost word perfect. I heard them so often that now, more than seventy years later, I can repeat some of the more striking or poetic phrases from these tales.

An incident happened during one of the supper-time sessions that is worth recounting. The long stool that I always used had a round hole in the middle of it for inserting a finger and picking it up. My father sat astride one end and I sat astride the other, with the plate of porridge and the bowl of milk between us.

Now every schoolboy knows that there is only one 'correct' way to eat porridge, and that is to pick up about half a spoonful of hot porridge, dip the spoon carefully in the milk-bowl, taking up enough cold milk to fill the spoon, and then transfer this gourmet's titbit to the mouth.

At that time we had a highly intelligent ginger cat that must have been watching the supper-time routine with a designing eye, because imagine our surprise one evening, when, as I was ferrying a spoonful from bowl to mouth, a ginger paw suddenly appeared through the hole in the middle of the stool, and performed a hooking movement as if trying to snatch the porridge. We both exclaimed loudly at the cat's ingenuity. My father especially found it most diverting.

That ginger cat was a great hunter, and no grounded bird or creeping animal was safe from him. In fact I had heard a neighbour telling my father that he had been watching our cat lying stretched out and perfectly still on the strip of sand on the fringe of Loch a Bhaile, and that when an inquisitive seagull landed and sidled up to investigate he suddenly exploded in an agile spring at the bird.

I myself can certainly vouch for this animal's capacity for speedy action. After we had moved into the barn to live (a circumstance that I shall come to later) I devised a practical joke on this cat based on my observation of his hunting qualities. I had noticed that in the evenings he took up a position, relaxed but watchful, beneath a wooden platform on which rested the tubs and pails with our supplies of ready-to-use well water. This part of the barn was separated from the residential portion by a wooden partition, the door of which was usually left open. Leaving doors open is a traditional Hebridean custom!

I spent some time carefully constructing a model mouse that I was sure would look quite lifelike in the dim evening light of the lower barn. I used dark-grey wool and black cotton thread, and the finished decoy was a convincing creature with a head, a plump body and a long tail. There were no legs, but they were not necessary as a long black cotton thread was tied round the neck with the other end of it in my hand for remote control.

I managed to park the mouse in a strategic position behind one of the wooden stanchions supporting the platform for the water containers, and to lay the black cotton thread through the door of the dividing partition and along the clay floor: all without being observed.

Some time later when I had checked that the cat had taken up his usual position I sat on my stool on the far side of the fire, which was in the middle of the barn floor. My father was reading the *Stornoway Gazette*, my mother was knitting as usual, and the rest of the family were going about their own various pastimes.

I gave a tentative tug at the black cotton thread, heard a movement and then I pulled in earnest; but unfortunately the position that I had taken up on the far side of the fire brought the 'mouse' racing across the hearth and almost into the fire, followed by a miniature projectile of ginger fur that burst in hot pursuit through the door, across the floor and through the hearth.

A cloud of ashes and a shower of sparks went flying towards the roof, as my mother dropped her knitting and my father the *Gazette* with simultaneous startled exclamations:

From my mother, 'Ach de tha cearr air a chat?' – 'But what's wrong with the cat?'

From my father, 'A Dhia gle mi! Tha'n cat air a dhol as a rian!' – 'God help me! The cat's gone crazy!'

Then they realised that I was convulsed in an effort to suppress the laughter (somewhat nervous I must admit) that was surging up inside me.

'De rinn thu?' – 'What did you do?' asked my father.

Somewhat sheepishly I dangled the mouse on the end of its thread: my mother shook her head as if in despair, but I could see she was smiling; my widely grinning chuckling father examined the 'mouse', but couldn't disguise the fact that he admired my ingenuity as he admonished me with, 'An anm ni math cur sin air falbh mas dean thu call' – 'In the name of goodness put that away before you cause a disaster.'

My education was proceeding very satisfactorily. At

school I was learning the mechanics of writing, counting and reading, and at home, after the serious beginning made in religious knowledge and memory training by my mother, my father was continuing with the more poetic and imaginative aspects of learning.

At school I could read the sequence of English sentences in the book provided for practice but I could not speak English. In retrospect I think that the part of my education that was going on at home was equally or even more valuable.

I have said that I couldn't speak English: nor could I speak Scots, as was borne out when I was accosted by an Aberdeen boy of my own age who was holidaying with his grandmother in the village. He approached with the obvious intention of friendly play, and in extrovert city manner opened the conversation with a flood of 'braid Scots'.

He might as well have been talking Chinese, and as he went on speaking I stood with downcast eyes trailing a toe in the dust of the road. It must have been the ultimate in lack of communication – a Doric-speaking Aberdonian and a Gaelic-speaking Hebridean. At last the poor lad turned away in disgust, exclaiming, 'Awa hame, ye black loon, ye canna speak!'

Of course I had no idea what he had said, but my mother who had been watching and listening told the story many times.

During the war years, with a steady income from my father's navy pay and with the benefits of the croft – potatoes, vegetables, milk, home-made butter, crowdie, cream, eggs and the ever-present standby of salt herrings – we were living rather well, setting up a strong basis for enduring later deprivations. There were of course the usual wartime shortages, but looking back I sometimes feel sure that the young in rural Lewis benefited for the rest of their lives from doing without certain things from 1914 to 1919.

I remember my brother John and I going to one of the village shops sometime after the war was over. I stayed outside while he went in for the message for which he had been sent, and when he came out he had something in his hand that I had never seen before. So I asked: 'De th'agad na do lamh?' '*Tha* toffee,' he replied. I then said, 'De th'ann toffee?' In English the conversation was 'What have you got in your hand?' 'It's a toffee.' 'What is a toffee?'

On another occasion my father came back from Stornoway with the horse and cart – he was carting to and from Stornoway whenever he could get a load – and my mother started cooking a meal when he got home. Gazing in complete puzzlement at the things on the frying pan I asked, 'De tha sin air a phraipean?' – 'What is that on the frying pan?' To which my father replied with a Rabelaisian chuckle, 'Tha boganan dearg!'

'*Tha* sausages!' – very emphatically – from my mother, not quite knowing whether to laugh or scowl at my father's bawdy response.

The things on the pan, that I had never seen before, were ordinary beef sausages.

And in that environment, was there room for relaxation? There were very few organised village sports, and most activities consisted of a group of youths getting together to have a go at putting the shot (the shot being a suitably sized and weighted round stone), the long jump, the hop-step and jump, and the occasional race. But these activities were limited. Too much had to be done in spring, summer and autumn.

An activity that was engaged in was dancing. This could be a barn dance or a road dance; the barn dance was usually quite well organised. Two or three village worthies would get together, approach a crofter who could make a barn available and get local pipers and accordion players to agree to provide the music. Then word was passed round advertising the projected entertainment. Anyone in the village who wished to go was welcome. They danced the night long, sometimes until five or six in the morning – quadrilles, lancers, eightsome reels, military two-steps, strip-the-willow, the *Washington Post* and so on. You had to be physically fit to last out a good-going barn dance.

The road dance was a much simpler affair and usually consisted of a group of young men and women who found themselves in the right place at the right time – a bridge or a crossroads – with a musician present. Someone would say, 'Let's have a dance!' and that would be it. The piper or accordion player would strike up and the fun would commence. Some of the young men would still be wearing their working boots and striking sparks off the stones in the roadway with their tackets. There was no tarmac in those days and seldom if ever was a dance interrupted by traffic. It was great fun.

I think however that the most relaxing part of Hebridean life was the *ceilidh*. The day's work was done, the peat-fire was glowing and a group of neighbours would gather in one of the houses. The original *ceilidh* was quite different from its modern counterpart, which takes the form of a concert of Gaelic songs, and is usually held in a concert hall or some similar accommodation; the original *ceilidh* was held in a thatched cottage by the peat-fire. There could and there would be a number of *ceilidhs* going on at the same time, in different houses, with the immediate neighbours participating in each case.

There would be reminiscences which would originate because the teller thought they might be entertaining. And they invariably were. The former merchant seaman would take his listeners to seaports all over the world. The member of the local Grazings Committee would report on decisions taken, never forgetting to report on amusing incidents that had happened at the meetings. Any and everybody was prepared to talk authoritatively on international politics, national politics and local politics: the county councillor was in there with Kaiser Wilhelm and Lloyd George.

Then someone would say, 'Come on now! That's enough! Let's have a song', and there was always someone ready to oblige. Then any new Gaelic poem would be recited or sung, and inevitably, as the visitors to the *ceilidh* house prepared to go home in the dark, there would be ghost stories.

After a day's work the croft-house *ceilidh* was not only entertainment, it was a relaxing psychological preliminary to bed.

6

No croft

IN 1920 THERE WAS another addition to the family with
the arrival of a second sister. Immemorial usage had to
be observed and she was named Johanna, this being the
girl's name nearest to that of my father's brother John,
who had been lost on the *Iolaire* the previous year. My
uncle Findlay went even further and named his daughter
Johnina.

There were now seven of us to feed and clothe –
mother, father, three sons and two daughters – and the
post-war depression was overtaking us with disconcerting speed.

The first really devastating blow that struck was when
my father discovered that he had to abandon the croft.
He himself was a younger one of six sons, so he had no
inheritance on the family estate, which consisted of a
stony croft in Bragar: when he had married my mother he
moved into her family croft in Shawbost where she lived
with her mother and father. She was the younger of two
daughters and there were no sons, so the older sister, who

was married in another part of the village, had inherited the croft on the death of my grandfather. Now that her husband was also home from the war, they wanted, quite rightly, to take over.

Once the position became clear to my father he began to make the barn on the croft habitable, and the family moved in, although my Auntie Mary's husband, John Macaulay, had told my father that he could occupy the house until he obtained other accommodation. In fact, though the house was left empty for him he didn't move in until we had found another place and had moved out of the barn. John Macaulay ('an Ban) was a gentle, considerate and inoffensive man.

It was about this time that a huge whale was washed ashore at Bragar, two miles away. The jawbone, which now forms an arch over a gate to the house 'Lakefield', measures twenty feet from the base to the apex, from which hangs the harpoon that was removed from the carcass. This mammal's vital statistics were eighty-two feet from nose to centre of tail, eighteen feet from tip to tip across the tail, with a diameter of twenty-four feet. A magnificent creature. It is not surprising that it escaped from the men who harpooned it.

The size of this brute was almost matched by the gigantic smell that emanated from it and permeated the locality, but in spite of this crofters came from far and near to cut out chunks of the blubber. These were put into tubs, barrels or whatever containers were available and then carted away for reducing to whale oil.

My father, who was cursed or blessed – depending on where he was standing – with a hypersensitive nose (which I have inherited) was always squeamish in the presence of a bad smell; notwithstanding, he went for a share of the blubber.

I shall always remember the reduction process: a fireplace of stones was prepared on the croft and a huge peat-fire was lit, with plenty of peats handy to keep it going. A large, black three-legged pot was set on the fire and pieces of the blubber were put into it; as these melted a stick was used to stir the smelly mess. My father stood to windward of the fire with his head turned away, stirring the contents of the pot while swearing quietly and comprehensively between the retching spasms that brought tears to his eyes – but we got our whale oil.

My great-uncle Calum occupied a nearby croft and I was on hand when he was extracting the oil. What I remember about the process is his son Kenneth dipping a stick in the pot and carefully smearing oil on his fine black leather shoes, his father remonstrating with him and saying, 'These shoes will never take polishing again,' and Kenneth replying: 'Perhaps not, but they won't let the water in either. Whale oil is the best treatment there is for leather.'

I have no knowledge of the purposes for which the crofters used the oil, but I do recollect my uncle Finlay telling my father that he was putting a small quantity of it into the mash that he was feeding to a calf, and that the beast was thriving.

We were now living in the barn and that was really going back to the primitive, with a peat-fire in the middle of the floor, on which all the cooking was done, and the eye-stinging peat-smoke escaping through a hole in the thatch, but not before it had us all in tears. Mercifully the curtain of oblivion that seems to protect the human mind from the harsher implications of environmental pressures came down once again and shut out the memory of almost all the time that we lived there.

The housing situation was impossible and my mother

made repeated trips by bus to Stornoway, both time-consuming and expensive, where she approached the proprietors of unfurnished lets recommended to her by her contacts. When it came to house-hunting, however, five children, of whom four were under ten years of age, were almost an insurmountable handicap.

The sheep (my father had started to build up a flock when he came home from the war), the milking cow and the horse had been sold when we abandoned the croft; and the money from these sales was fast running out, if it had not already done so.

7

Coulregrein

ONE DAY my mother came back from Stornoway with the news that there was one room available for occupation in a little cottage on Sand Street in the village of Coulregrein. The living space was utterly inadequate – the whole cottage would have been inadequate for a family of seven – but my parents decided to make the move. There was nothing for them in Shawbost, but so near the town there would always be some chance of work for a willing strong workman. My father was thirty-nine.

The excitement generated by the move was soon dampened by the living conditions. The one room where the seven of us had to wash, cook, eat, live and sleep was so small that it would not hold two beds; not if there was to be room for a table and a shelved box for cooking and eating utensils. My father solved the problem by telescoping the two iron bedsteads so that the head rails were against the two end walls, with a communal foot-rail in between.

Looking back I can never hope to understand how we all lived inside that little box. Fortunately once again I have little recollection of what went on inside the house: my memories of Sand Street are almost entirely of things that happened outside, and they are very happy.

One memory I do have of inside is all seven of us being down with flu at the same time – and in that restricted space believe me we plumbed the depths of misery. The school attended by Coulregrein children at that time was Laxdale Public School where iron discipline was maintained with the aid of a leather strap with its 'fingers' dangling carried in the headmaster's hip pocket and always referred to by him as 'the lion's tail'. He was known to us as Thor – the God of Thunder. Scholastically there were two passions in his life: music and arithmetic. If you were good at music you could almost get away with not being good at arithmetic, and if you were good at arithmetic you could almost get away with not being good at music, but if you were good at neither you were living on borrowed time.

In Shawbost the everyday language had been Gaelic, but in Laxdale it was English, and as I really couldn't speak English with any degree of facility I found the transition difficult. One learns quickly at that age, however, and I made reasonable progress, especially when I got into the classes taken by Miss Maclennan. She was an absolute genius. Of all the teachers that I ever knew, primary, elementary, secondary and university, there is only one other that I would put in the same bracket with her, and that is Norman B. Anderson, who was English master in my time in the Nicolson Institute.

There were two grades in the classroom in which she taught, but she did not need a 'lion's tail' to maintain discipline: we were disciplined by the respect in which we held her. I went into her first grade fumbling my way into some familiarity with a foreign language, English, and less than two years later, before I left her second grade, I had read all the books in the class library and she was very generously bringing me books from her own library at home. I owe her a deep debt of gratitude.

When living on Sand Street one of our ploys was to go home from school for our lunch break, if the tide was suitable, across the *fideach*, the salt flats between Coulregrein and the mouth of the Laxdale river. We went as a group and made a race of it, keeping the course as near as possible to 'as the crow flies' – in the Laxdale road, a beeline through some Laxdale crofts, across the *fideach*, a leap across the *draine mhor* (the big drain) – then a break-off by the Cross Street boys while the Sand Street boys carried on across more crofts.

Those who broke off for Cross Street were Paddy-a-Dick, Deelah, Ginger Morrison and Willie Robb. On to Sand Street went Fatty Fraser, Murdo Knox, Iain Mor (my brother) and Safety (myself). We all had our nicknames and would have been startled if addressed by our proper names: only teachers did that.

There could not have been much of a meal when we did get home: the distance was too long and the time too short. It was a case of a sip and a bite of whatever was going, and then the race back to school. Our fuel intake was so meagre and our energy expenditure so great that it is surprising we didn't do ourselves permanent injury.

When not at school we played on the sands of the Cockle Ebb when the tide was out, or in the whin bushes below Goathill Farm; or we made our way to the football park in Goathill to play, or to spectate if there was a match in progress. The 'gate money' in those days consisted of whatever voluntary contributions went into a collecting box that was taken round and shaken hopefully in front of the spectators by some dedicated committee member. We poverty-stricken youngsters were not expected to contribute, and did our watching free.

All the water used at home was taken from a gushing crystal spring below Goathill Farm, and fetching buckets of it for domestic use was one of my chores, as was the collection of sticks for kindling. I resented both of these chores very much when they interfered with my arrangements for play.

There was a shoemaker working on Sand Street and I spent a lot of time in his wooden shed watching him at work. This proved very useful in the future when I mended my own boots, and then found that I had to mend boots for other members of the family as well.

Sometimes he sent me into town to deliver mended boots and shoes to customers, or even to buy leather for his cobbling. But money was scarce: many people were reduced to mending their own footwear. Custom-made boots or shoes were a luxury that no-one could afford, and the shoemaker, James (Jimmy Osh) Macleod was another ex-serviceman who left his native island on the *Metagama* exodus to Canada.

At the lower end of Sand Street lived the Frasers. They had two huge horses and lorries that were engaged in Stornoway during the two open fishing seasons for transporting wooden kits of herrings from piers to curing stations. Naturally I gravitated towards the stables, admiring the beautiful horses (many prize tickets from local shows were pinned to their stalls) with their shining black leather harnesses and polished brasses. Access to this world of stables and horses was made available by John Roddy (Fatty) Fraser, with whom I spent a lot of time playing football, sparring and participating in the usual run of schoolboy activities.

Outside the stables were large wooden barrels, containing an exotic mixture, mostly cereals for feeding the horses. Fatty showed me a certain constituent of this mixture (if I remember correctly he called it 'locusts') that he ate and which, when I tried it, I found sweet and palatable.

We were constantly delving into the barrels to supplement our diet with this delicacy, and although Duncan Fraser just grinned when he saw us at it, sometimes Old Man Fraser, Fatty's grandfather, would give a good-natured growl of discouragement. But once his back was turned we were back at the barrels.

Sometimes on his way back from town after a long tiring day of carting Duncan Fraser would stop at our house on his way past to leave a fry of kippers, and I remember that on one occasion he left a whole box.

While living on Sand Street I spent more time at play with Fatty than with anyone in the village. Later he joined the Seaforth Highlanders and was killed in Italy.

A memory of that village that I cherish is of the horse-drawn baker's van doing its rounds, and of the spicy mouth-watering aroma of fresh baking when the van doors were opened. This was something that I had never experienced before moving to Coulregrein.

In spite of the abject living conditions in our box-room slum we were a happy family and could always have laughter and fun, however adverse the circumstances.

Uncle Finlay, my father's brother, came all the way from Bragar to visit us on a number of occasions while we were at Sand Street. He was deeply religious and was a genuinely good man. As soon as he sat down, on every occasion that he called, a religious discussion began, and although I understood little of what was going on I was impressed by the flow of language. When I was old enough to understand in later years it was like being at a debate between two practised theologians: both were so well versed in their subject, and both could quote so convincingly and so eloquently endorse their arguments.

I am sure that apart from brotherly love one of the main reasons why uncle Finlay came to Coulregrein, and later to all the other houses in which we lived, was for the benefit of these discussions with my father.

I remember a cousin of mine telling me in Glasgow that one of the things he liked, when he went to the Shawbost Free Church while on holiday in Bragar, was hearing my uncle Finlay at prayer – 'It is as if he were having a private conversation with God.'

The discussions moved at times from the religious to the political stage, as my father was an enthusiastic socialist, and the depressed conditions obtaining throughout the country, especially in the Hebrides, provided plenty of scope for critical comment and for suggesting an alternative strategy.

I recall going into Stornoway one Saturday evening and standing at the rails outside Perceval Square where a small company of travelling entertainers were putting on a show. The stage consisted of a platform of boards set on top of upended herring barrels. The box-office was a box – but no office – which was taken round by a member of the cast. I remember the colourful make-up on the faces – it was my first experience of live theatre – but nothing of the show itself apart from a recurring cynical refrain after each verse of one of the ditties that they sang. It went:

Three cheers for the Red, White and Blue.
Are you working? No! Are you?

They must have been ex-servicemen.

8

Laxdale

———————

WE JUST COULD NOT go on living as we were doing, and my mother was ever on the hunt for other accommodation. This time the place she found was in Laxdale, a fairly standard house of the time, two rooms up, two down: there were two windows downstairs, one on each side of the only door, and two upstairs. Each gable-end had a fireplace, and built on to one gable was a structure with a corrugated iron roof – the barn and byre combined. The nearest outside toilet was a municipal one in Stornoway, about a mile away; there was of course no plumbing in our house. The landlady lived upstairs: our family of seven lived in the two downstairs rooms, and we had the use of a plot between the house and the road for planting potatoes and vegetables. The fact that the wooden floor was rotting away, and that you had to be careful where to put a foot in case of a sprained ankle or even a broken leg, was a mere trifle, however, and not worth considering in relation to the more important fact of increased living space – from one room to two.

For light, we relied upon paraffin lamps: in those days there was, of course, neither electricity nor gas, and candles were not used a great deal. The grossly inadequate sanitary arrangements focused upon the chamber pot or the byre, depending on the where and the when.

I was now eleven years old and had begun to be a bit of help about the place. A friend had given us some peat banks on the far side of the Tong road beyond the Blackwater bridge. There I helped with the turfing, the cutting, the lifting, and later the ferrying to the roadside for taking home by cart. On one occasion when we ran short I went from Rudha 'n Fhitheich to the far side of the Blackwater river and took home a bag of peats on my back before going to school in the morning; quite a marathon for an eleven-year-old who had only narrowly escaped becoming a digit in the infant mortality statistics on three separate occasions before he was five.

Part of this time my father was working in the grounds of Lewis Castle, clearing up fallen trees, of which there were many hundreds after one of our more spectacular Hebridean storms, and he could take home for his own use as much as he could carry on his shoulder. What he could carry all the way from the castle policies to Laxdale was as much as ordinary men could lift. In fact one of his neighbours, a big powerful man who was working with him, confessed when talking to a friend that he had frequently wished to take a turn of carrying the load of firewood, but was afraid that if my father put it down he wouldn't be able to lift it.

During the dinner hour, when the other workmen were resting, he sawed lengths of wood almost through at about 8–10-inch intervals; he then bound the lengths with a rope, ready for hoisting on to his shoulder when he finished in the evening. When he got home all that he had to do was to knock the timbers against a large stone in front of the house and so break off 8–10-inch logs. This was a useful and economical supplement to our fuel requirements – economical in money terms, although the payment in toil and sweat was high. Although not a tall man my father was 13 stone of squat bone and muscle, was tremendously strong, and possessed of explosive energy.

It was while living in Laxdale that my brother John successfully sat a bursary examination for entrance to a secondary education at the Nicolson Institute. I still remember how self-conscious he was going off that morning, and no wonder, because, in an effort to appear respectably dressed in the examination room, he was wearing the suit in which his father had been married. A suit which, although still immaculate, was more than a trifle dated. For size John could wear it comfortably; he was big for his age and was known in Laxdale School as Iain Mor – Big John.

My father set great store by education and was determined that any member of the family who showed the ability to benefit from further study should be given the opportunity to do so. On a labourer's wage, when he was lucky enough to be employed, he could have done with sending out a big, strong oldest son to earn a few extra shillings to help the family, but he never for one moment considered doing so. John was doing well at school and he must be given every chance of further advancement.

It was in this house too that the twins were born into the family, a girl and a boy. The girl was named Annabella – her mother's name – and the boy Kenneth Murdo. While in Coulregrein we had got news that my father's brother, Uncle Kenneth, had been killed by a fall while working as a spiderman on a construction job in Canada. Custom dictated that his brother's next child should be given his name, and my mother insisted on including my father's name – Murdo.

The twins were seven-month babies, and nearly didn't survive, but once they got beyond the first precarious period they made good progress. They were premature because my mother couldn't let a mere trifle like advanced pregnancy interfere with her sense of purpose. She did what she thought needed doing.

The day I was born she had been gathering seaweed and had taken a creel of the stuff home on her back; the day my sister Mary was born the labour pains began while she was on the way home with a creel of peats; the day the twins were born she had taken the raw materials for making black-and-white puddings from the abattoir in Coulregrein, and then she had cleaned the lot in the clear-running water of the Laxdale river which was not polluted in those days. She was thirty-nine years of age, so it is not surprising in the circumstances that there was a premature confinement.

Now there were nine of us: mother, father, three daughters and four sons. There was no extra money coming in and there was no additional living space. Besides, some friction had developed, the details of which I never knew, between our landlady, who lived upstairs in the house, and my mother. The search for a house was on once more.

9

Newvalley

Odd jobs

This time the move was to a thatched two-roomed cottage in Newvalley. The rooms were smaller than the ones we left, but there were no holes in the floor – it was made of clay. There was a fairly commodious stone-built peat-shed with a tarred felt roof, and at the back of the house a wooden hen-shed.

Peat banks in the Cnoc Mor went with the house, as did a plot of ground. There were, of course, no toilet facilities and all water had to be carried in buckets from the neighbouring well. For occupation by a family of nine it couldn't be described as anything other than a rural slum, but we were happy there.

If there is one thing that I shall ever be grateful for it is that wherever we lived, however abject the conditions or stringent the economic circumstances, we were a happy family, with laughter always bubbling below the surface and needing little encouragement to break out. My family survived, like all Islanders, because of perpetual hard work on the land and sea, and because of the system of mutal communal aid that obtained at the time.

For me the years that I spent in Newvalley from 1924 until 1933 were among the most significant in my life. There were so many colourful characters and so much was happening. There may have been, and in fact there were, many frustrating moments, but there was never a dull one.

A chore that I performed regularly while staying at Laxdale was fetching water for a next-door neighbour; but this was no ordinary water carrying. The water in the wells near at hand, although clean and adequate, did not compare with the sweet crystal-clear coolness of that from Tobair (well) Alaic 'an Tailleir; this spring was situated at the top of a croft in Guershader, and even in the driest summer weather there was water in it. Each day after school I set out from Rudha 'n Fhitheich with a large white enamel pail and a tin mug. The journey with the empty pail was a long strenuous uphill climb, and although the homeward journey was downhill I was carrying water, and had to be extremely careful how I carried it or most of it would be lost through spillage. The whole performance was tiring, and there was the added frustration of time lost from play.

When we moved to Newvalley I thought that I had finished my time as a water-carrier. Alas for youthful hopes; Mrs Morrison wanted me to carry on with the daily routine and I couldn't refuse. Each evening after I delivered the water I took the empty pail back with me to Newvalley, so that I could take it direct to the well in Guershader and then on to Laxdale.

This was only one of many tasks that I had to perform, and when I look back I sometimes wonder that I had any time for play.

The focal point in all rural households at that time was the peat-fire, and a standard practice was to put a *ceap* or wedge of turf at the back of the fire. This meant that less peats were used, the heat was thrown out into the room, and the *ceap* dried as the fire was replenished and was itself consumed.

One of the jobs that I got directly after going to Newvalley was to produce a barrowload of turf for one of the neighbours each Saturday morning. This meant setting off with a barrow and spade, cutting enough slabs of turf to fill the barrow, then wheeling the load back to the village. For this I got sixpence (2½ pence in today's currency). Not a princely sum, but the exact entrance fee to Will Mack's Picture House on Keith Street in Stornoway.

Sometimes too Murdo (The Nipper) Maciver would ask me to go out with him to help fill the cart if he had to fetch a load of peats, and that usually meant another sixpence although I would gladly have done it for nothing because of the ride in the cart.

Murdo was working for Donald (Domhnull Mor) Ross, who stayed two houses away from us, and he was 'living in'. I am certain that the wage he was getting in these days was such that a sixpence out of it for me was exceedingly generous. He joined the Royal Naval Reserve while at Domhnull Mor's and then went into the Merchant Navy; sadly in the early 1930s he was washed overboard and lost in the North Sea. The news of his death, which reached me in Glasgow where I was a student at the time, hit me like a personal bereavement.

As time went on and I got older, bigger and stronger the tasks became more numerous and more remunerative. There was one that I did for some considerable time for which I got paid, although I got no money.

We were then getting all our grocery and bakery requirements from Murdo Morrison's in Bayhead, and meeting the weekly bill for such a large family out of a labourer's meagre wage, or out of his dole money, was well nigh impossible. As a way of making this easier it was suggested by Mr Morrison that I should assist in the bakery on Saturday mornings from 8 a.m. to 1 p.m., with my earnings to be set against the week's bill. This was what I did, and it was quite an experience.

On arriving at work in the morning I was given a white apron like the other bakers; and my first task each week was to clean the inside of the mechanical dough-mixer with a metal scraper and then to oil it ready for use the following week. That done I was given general duties to perform: sieving flour, kneading bread, filling and lidding meat pies, glazing buns, washing down surfaces, sweeping the floor, shovelling coke, in fact anything that had to be done of which it was thought I was capable.

Above the bakehouse there was a store to which I was sent occasionally to tidy up. Access was by a set of concrete steps and an end door. There was also a side door leading on to a catwalk that connected with a joiner's workshop across the alley.

This workshop was run by Mr Morrison's brother, who did a small sideline as an undertaker, and sometimes a spare coffin found its way across to the place where I tidied up, for storage purposes.

Once Saturday morning Mr Morrison came in as I was looking at one of these coffins which was lying open with the lid on one side.

'That's a fine coffin,' he said.

'It certainly is,' I agreed.

'Try it on, Johnnie boy,' he continued.

'What do you mean, try it on?' I asked.

'Lie down in it, to see if it will fit you' – with a twinkle in his eye.

'Not on your life!' I responded. 'You'd put the lid on and screw me down just for the hell of it!'

He then shuffled away, chuckling gleefully at his own macabre humour. Kenny (Lux) Maclean was the foreman baker and his assistant was Alexander Donald (Krooge) Nicolson: he would stand very straight, throw out his chest and declaim in ringing tones, when any of us youngsters called him Krooge: 'My name is Nicolson, Alexander Donald.' Malcolm (Salution) Macdonald was the apprentice. Murdo (Warhorse) Morrison, the master baker himself, was always there, and everything in that bakehouse went with a cheerful, at times even hilarious, swing. He was a dedicated Labour Party supporter, and there were arguments, discussions, criticisms, counter-criticisms, quips and banter. It was lively and stimulating.

When the regular bakery staff went off for breakfast I was left alone with some task to do until they came back. Mr Morrison would come in with a bottle of lemonade, scones and/or cakes and say, 'There you are Johnnie boy, sit down and have that while the others are at breakfast.'

He called everyone 'Johnnie boy' quite indiscriminately: his foreman baker, the journeyman, the apprentice, myself – whomever he had occasion to address.

He was full of generous impulses. The lemonade and cakes were always free. And at times during the week on my way home from school he would beckon to me across the street, take me into the bakeshop, and pointing to a tray of hot meat pies fresh from the oven, would say, 'Take one of these Johnnie Boy to eat going out the road.' And they were the best meat pies in Stornoway: the freshly minced steak was taken from the neighbouring butcher's shop just before the pies were got ready for the oven, and the foreman baker attended personally to the mixing and seasoning, and supervised the filling of the pies.

When the baking tray came out of the oven with the finished articles the first pies that came off the tray were for the foreman baker to take home for his own family's use. So they had to be good.

On Saturday nights, when people took home the week-end groceries, no one left his shop with an empty basket or creel whether or not they could pay. But he found in the end that his mistaken brand of benevolent practical socialism could not work within the framework of a rapacious capitalist economy, and he went bankrupt.

Incidentally it was Murdo (Warhorse) Morrison who introduced me to Robert Tressell's *The Ragged Trousered Philanthropists* by lending me a copy.

Day-work

It was in the spring of 1927, before I was fifteen, that I was given my first day-work job. It was during the Easter holidays.

On the *obair latha* or day-work system you were engaged for and paid by the day – usually from 8 a.m. until 6 p.m., with short breaks for breakfast, dinner and tea – and the going rate then for men was five shillings (25p today) a day plus the three meals referred to above.

This, my first venture, was the rather messy and unsavoury one of transferring manure in barrow-loads from dung-heap to croft. By now I had developed some considerable expertise in the use of the barrow, and although on a Lewis croft at that time of year the going was soft and difficult I was able to cope so successfully that after I had finished the job, which lasted if I remember for three days, I was given a full man's wage by a grateful employer.

The following summer holidays (I was fifteen in May) a neighbour asked me whether I was prepared to do day-work at ferrying peats. I agreed; and again, and on all future occasions, drew a full man's wage for every full day worked. I found out later that my employer for the peat-ferrying had asked my employer of the Easter holidays what wage to pay me – after all I was only a fifteen-year-old boy – and was told, 'Give him a man's wage. You won't find any man who will better him with a barrow.'

The very next spring I was engaged on another croft on the same task of barrowing manure. This time there were two of us and my partner was that rough but engaging character Calum (Fox) Macdonald. He was a strong, dour, steady worker.

The manure was smelly, moist and heavy, and the going was squelchy and difficult. When we started after breakfast I was loading my barrow forkful for forkful with him, and finding it a testing task to keep up with him. After the dinner break, by the middle of the afternoon, he was having his work cut out to keep up with me.

Overlooking the croft on which we worked were the heights of Benside, from where there was virtually a bird's eye view of Newvalley. So when the going got really tough and exhausting by the late afternoon Calum paused and grunted gruffly, 'Now take it easy! The people of Benside will be watching, and if you keep up this pace they'll have us up there barrowing shit for the rest of the spring!'

Calum was a rough diamond, but running through the roughness there was a warmth that sometimes showed in strange ways. More than once on payday or dole day he came back from town with two strings of haddocks, one of which he handed in at our door.

Now well launched on the *obair latha* circuit I could usually find plenty of work; during the Easter holidays at croft-work and peat cutting, and during the summer holidays peat-ferrying from banks to roadside for taking home by cart. Because I was engaged on those tasks for people all over the village the same kind of work that had to be done for our own household was done on a spare-time basis, in the evenings, or on Saturday afternoons when my father was home from work.

It was invariably fun to work with my father. I was not big and was lightly built, but possessed the same kind of explosive energy that he had himself, although nothing like his strength. On occasion I brought this explosiveness into play with dire consequences. Turfing banks for peat-cutting in the Cnoc Mor you could come across a really unyielding patch, and my father maintained that I broke a spade every spring. He would shake his head and say, 'Tha iomradh as a ramh gun a bhriseadh' – 'There is rowing in the oar without breaking it.'

When cutting the peats, if I came across a fibrous patch through which it was difficult to drive the blade of the iron I leapt at it, so as to get all my weight into play, with the result that both my feet were off the ground as my right foot drove down on to the wooden step of the cutter. In the throwing position below me, my father, would exclaim, 'A dhia gle mi! C'air son a tha thu danns air an tairsgiar?' – 'God help me. Why are you dancing on the peat-iron?' But we always worked well together.

Sometimes a little light relief was introduced when my brother John and myself would engage in friendly bouts of sparring, wrestling, or (a favourite) the standing broad jump. As John was an inch and a half taller than I and about a couple of stone heavier I sometimes had to use rather devious means of trying to hold my own. In his tolerant good-natured way John would put up with my tricks, but my father, although he would laugh at some of my ways of trying to avoid catastrophe (especially in the wrestling), always insisted that the strictest rules of fair play must be observed. Only he never said 'fair play' but used the expression – whether at the time he was talking in Gaelic or English – *Cothrom na Feinne*. This was the code of the Fingalians, and simply stated it means that in all contests and at all times you must extend to your opponent every advantage that you would expect for yourself. It was an attitude that has contributed in great measure to my enjoyment of all the sports and games in which I have participated since.

We made a habit of taking with us a piece of soap and a towel, as some of our peat banks were close by the Laxdale river, and even if there was no pool big enough or deep enough for much swimming, at least we could have a bath. The lack of space did not dampen our enthusiasm and we had a great time splashing about in the water. The river provided our only means of having a proper bath.

When we had cut and dried our own peats we ferried them to the roadside and stacked them, as we couldn't afford to pay to have them carted home. So most of the peats that we burned were taken by barrow from the Cnoc Mor to Newvalley.

During the holidays, Easter, summer and Christmas, there were plenty opportunities for getting a few barrow-loads home, but when not on holiday things were different and somewhat of a penance. For years my first task on getting home from school was to pick up the barrow and set off to the roadside stack for peats. Something that I could put up with in fine weather, and even enjoy. However, in excessively wet weather when the iron wheel kept sinking and sticking in the sodden clay, or when I had to push through snow I found it very frustrating. But I was never cold doing that job: even climbing up the brae to the Cnoc Mor with an empty barrow could produce a sweat.

Sometimes Donald (Domhnull Mor) Ross would come over to the house and say to my mother 'If you have peats at the road I'll get Murdo to go out with the horse and cart to take home a load; if you'll get the boy to go out with him to fill the cart.' When my mother protested that she couldn't pay for such a service he would say 'That's all right. The next time that I go to the moors perhaps the boy will come with me to help with the sheep.' The 'Boy' for both cart-filling and sheep-chasing was I. When he went moor-trotting after his sheep he took me with him instead of a dog, conceivably he laid the foundation for my subsequent small success as a long-distance runner.

These occasional carts of peats were a great boon, providing a reassuring standby for the occasions when the use of the barrow was impossible.

When I worked at his peats, which I did several summers, he would say to me with a twinkle in his eye and a quirk at the corner of his mouth, 'Don't put so much in the barrow – but run with it' – 'Na bi cuir uiread as a bhara – ach bi na da ruith!'

Domhnull Mor was a good neighbour. He would come to the door with a pail of potatoes or a bottle of fresh milk and say to my mother, 'Put that away quickly in case Maggie sees it' – Maggie was his wife – 'and I'll get the pail (or the bottle) again.'

I shall have more to say about Domhull Mor later.

The peats

One of the places where a deal of the village peats were cut was the nearly level top of Bennadrove and I spent many tiring but nonetheless enjoyable days working there. The views from the perimeter of the plateau were magnificent in all directions, although we had little 'time to stand and stare'.

As this was summer work we frequently took off our boots and socks as soon as we arrived at the banks, making for more agile movement among the tussocks and clumps through which the barrows had to be manoeuvred. A feature of working in this location was that pulling the empty barrow back up the hill from the roadside was as exhausting as taking it down full.

In a wet season when the ground was soft the wheel sometimes sank to the axle in the peat. It couldn't be pushed forward, and rather than struggle backwards the method used for getting out was to push a knee under the back of the barrow press hard down on the shafts using the knee as a fulcrum for raising the wheel, slew the front of the barrow sideways to get the wheel on to hard ground. The energy expended on this operation was more fatiguing than the remainder of the journey to the road. Each summer I had blue lines of bruises across both thighs just above the knees as a result of these efforts.

Nevertheless we had a lot of fun as many of us working there were young enough to laugh in the most impossible circumstances – as the Lewis saying has it, 'Our hearts were in the tops of our heads.'

A man with whom I spent many days on Bennadrove

was Donald (Dodie) Macpherson. What a worker he was: lean and wiry, and tough as a steel spring, he would work his heart out all day and then after tea walk into Stornoway to do a stint unloading the mail boat as a member of the dock's casual labour squad.

He had a wry sense of humour and would keep me amused with his quiet comments on some of the things that went on around us on the hill. There was one character whom he always referred to as 'Noon', because, Dodie maintained, he never appeared at his peats on Bennadrove until midday.

Among the highlights of peat work was eating out of doors. We usually had breakfast before setting off in the morning, but by dinner time, with the clean moor air and the exercise, we were ravenous. There would be a huge peat-fire blazing, started with dry heather for kindling, in a strategic position beside a carefully chosen level grassy area, where a tablecloth was set and held in position by stones placed at its corners. We took up our positions round the cloth, either squatting on the grass or sitting on a couple of peats.

The food was always wholesome and plentiful, and if it did have a flavour of peat-smoke that was something to which we were long accustomed in our own homes. I have tasted peat-smoke off crowdie, home-made butter, and even a boiled egg that came from a blackhouse, but they were none the worse for that.

In addition to the five shillings a day that I was earning on day-work when available, and a fair proportion of which was used for kitting me out for school, I also supplemented the family income by making forays into the Stornoway harbour area during the fishing seasons to collect herrings. These could be got by taking up a strategic stance in relation to the baskets, swinging from drifter to quay. As the baskets swung the odd herring inevitably fell out, and there was a tacit understanding between the fishermen, the curers' workmen and the waiting boys that the falling herrings were fair pickings.

In those days before greedy, intensive, all-the-year-round fishing had nearly destroyed our herring stocks fishermen were practical conservationists by tradition. In Stornoway there were two open fishing seasons, a short winter season and a long summer one, separated by two closed seasons. In the Moray Firth, the North Sea and off East Anglia, seasonal fishing was also practised. Furthermore fishing was by drift net, so that the smaller fish went through the mesh and could survive and develop.

Nowadays, sadly, in places where boys could once collect strings of herrings free of charge to feed hungry families, a herring has become a luxury.

Fortunately there were plenty available when I was young, and I have often thought that were it not for that availability many more families in the town of Stornoway and in the neighbouring villages would have been suffering from malnutrition. In our household, certainly, herring was the staple diet for a large part of the year, and especially during the sunnier months, when they were on the menu at least once, and sometimes twice a day, every day of the week except Sunday.

Play

After all that, where did the time come from for play? For play there was, pursued as energetically as work and a good deal more enthusiastically. In the winter evenings there were the ceilidhs by the fireside with the traditional mixture of tales, poems and songs. In our house the doyen of these ceilidhs was Domhnull Mor. He would knock on our door, always in the same way, with the crook of his stick: and when the door was opened his greeting was ever the same, ' 'S ann go du bhuanachd!' – 'This is for your benefit!' And indeed it was.

Once he had settled down by the fire and filled his pipe, frequently with tobacco proffered by my father out of his own carefully rationed supply, the stories would begin. So too would the poems and songs, for it was quite surprising in the course of how many tales he would say, 'And a poem was made up about this,' or 'A song was composed about that.' He would recite the poem or sing the song, possessed as he was of a prodigious memory and an ear for a tune. In his young days he had been a boon companion of *Tormod Beag nan Amhrain* (Little Norman of the Songs) a notable Lewis bard, and when they went together into the 'Imperial', one of the Stornoway inns, Tormod Beag would recite or sing for Domhnull Mor his most recent compositions. Domhnull, whose memory, as I have already said, was phenomenal, learned and remembered them. Now more than half a century later, we were sitting in a little thatched cottage in Newvalley enjoying the fruits of his association with the Bard. Listening to his performances – for performances they were – on these winter nights, was a rewarding aesthetic experience for his audience.

The regrettable truth is that a great many of the tales that he told, the verses that he recited and the songs that he sang died with him. They were lost to posterity because no effort was made to preserve them. I was too young to have the foresight to try to keep them alive against the day of his passing, and people who should have been storing these gems of Gaelic culture for future generations to enjoy were out of touch with the down-to-earth realities of an illiterate crofter's comprehensive memory.

When Domhnull died, we, to whom he had given so much, felt deprived as well as bereaved. I would like to think of him as striding through the heather of *Tir-nan-Og* in his patched tweeds, arm in arm with Tormod Beag, and both of them reciting Gaelic poetry and lustily singing Gaelic songs.

A house that I frequently visited on winter nights, and in fact all the year round, was Alec 'an Tailleir's in Guershader. Living here with his mother and three brothers was one of my classmates, Donald Duncan Mackinnon, who became a lifelong friend. There was a gramophone with a large and varied collection of records, and all night long the strains of music could be heard out on the road. When the gramophone was not playing John (Eoin) Martin entertained with selections on the accordion, or Dolly Mop (who died young of tuberculosis) played the mouth organ.

The noise, on which the young of every generation appear to thrive, must have been mind-boggling for adults, but I do not recall Donald Duncan's mother ever remonstrating with us or showing impatience. She was as generous towards our youthful excesses as she was in everything that she did.

Many years later, when I worked one winter as a temporary postman delivering letters in that district, she kept a lookout for me, and a hot cup of tea with something palatable to eat was ready and waiting for me when I reached her door. Whether or not there was mail for her I had to stop to have what she prepared, for who could refuse such warm generosity? This happened every single day all the time I was on that delivery.

There were no village halls in those days but we got our dancing done just the same, more often than not at some road-end to the music of an accordion. The conditions underfoot could be treacherous and didn't do our footwear any good, but we weren't wearing dancing pumps, and occasionally sparks would fly as a tackety boot came into uncoordinated contact with a flinty stone.

When there was a village wedding a barn would be provided for the wedding dance by a crofter who had a barn big enough and with a reasonably level floor; on these occasions there was usually a piper as well as an accordionist. There might be only one set of bagpipes but in that locality there were always present two or three who could play. The area – Laxdale, Guershader, Newvalley, Benside – was a nursery for pipers. They provided the music and we danced until dawn, even on the long winter nights, with strip-the-willows, dashing white sergeants, lancers, quadrilles, eightsome reels, military two-steps, foxtrots and waltzes; you had to be a trained athlete to last out the pace of a good-going barn dance from start to finish.

On frosty moonlit winter nights we walked in groups for miles, romping, singing, arguing and engaging in general harmless horseplay. We were not disturbed by traffic and could walk all night sometimes without passing a car. One occasion I recall there being such a severe frost that a friend, Norrie Murray from Laxdale Lane, and I went sliding on solid ice from pool to pool on the Laxdale river all the way from below the Newvalley crofts to its mouth.

Norrie was drowned on active service in the Royal Naval Patrol Service early in the war.

Another winter pastime was when a crofter took a cornstack into his barn for threshing and we were asked to lend a hand with turning the wheel of the hand-operated threshing mill.

There were two on the handle of the wheel that operated the toothed metal cylinder to which the sheaves of corn were fed. This was hard sweaty work, but as we were treated to a sumptuous meal when the work was done, and as it was winter when we were looking for ways of passing the time, we did not think of it as work; any invitation to a night threshing corn was accepted with alacrity.

There was a good municipal library in Stornoway, and we in the neighbouring communities, although outside the burgh, were permitted access if sponsored by a responsible ratepayer in the town. This sponsorship was readily available, and I certainly had no difficulty in getting the necessary form signed. This opened up a whole range of new territory to be explored and enjoyed, for, although a late starter, I had become an avid reader: so much so that I frequently had a book under my pillow and even read in the mornings before getting up to go to school. That was in summer time, of course, because in winter there was not enough light for reading so early.

So the town library provided another way of filling in the long dark nights of the Hebridean winter, when, as happened too often, gale-force winds and lashing rain prevented any outdoor activity. There was a very special pleasure in sitting with a good book in the radiant heat of a huge peat-fire while cold rain spattered the window and out of the deep darkness storm-winds moaned in the eaves.

A quite popular winter pastime among some of my friends was playing cards, but it was one for which I have never been able to generate any enthusiasm. Even in the navy, so many years later, when off-duty mess-deck life virtually revolved round the card-table I didn't participate, but found relaxation in a book, or writing letters.

Full as was the village life in winter, it was more so in spring, summer and autumn when the days were far too short to contain all our activities of work and play.

The first or most important game, as in nearly all of Scotland, was football. This we played in our early years with any kind of small ball that was available; a discarded tennis ball was a special dispensation of providence, and we fought out matches to a determined finish with nothing more elaborate than the cork from a herring net. A person who has never used this type of football would be surprised at how much dribbling and kicking technique can be put into playing with a cork. There were no goalposts or retaining nets; the target area was marked as being between two stones, or between players' discarded clothing in the form of jackets or jerseys. This gave rise to most of the arguments on the field, as there could be irreconcilable differences of opinion as to whether a shot had gone inside or outside imaginary uprights, under or over an imaginary crossbar, into or not into an imaginary net. But I have no recollection of anyone being ordered off.

As we got older we graduated to a real football, obtained by having a whip-round among enthusiasts. We couldn't play with any success in the school playground because it was so steep, and too often the ball went over the bottom wall into the Laxdale river; when this happened there was a crazy scramble over the wall and a race along the river bank in an attempt at early interception, but this could take some time, and the ball might be well down river before it was retrieved. These interruptions were most discouraging; furthermore the playground surface was unsuitable, being gravelly at the top and muddily soft at the bottom; we only used it during school playtime, and then reluctantly.

Once a year, on New Year's morning, a small delegation of final-year pupils went to the schoolhouse after breakfast; and, with mutual expressions of goodwill for the coming year, a brand new football was handed over by the headmaster. I do not know when this practice began, or for how long it was maintained, but this gift was made all the years that I was at Laxdale School. So we were always praying for a fine dry crisp day on New Year's morning, although even at that age we had some doubts about the efficacy of such an exercise.

Two playing areas were used, known as the 'little pitch' and the 'big pitch'. These were fairly level grassy patches of ground cut off by two loops of the river, one below the Laxdale crofts and the other near its mouth. To call either a pitch was an act of faith, based entirely on the substance of things hoped for.

When practising or playing among ourselves we used the little pitch as it was nearer; when it was an important match between the Lapps (Laxdale) and the Coolies (Coulregrein), or between the Lapps and the Bayheads (Bayhead Stornoway), then it was played on the big pitch with all the fervour of an international.

The big pitch was also used in the summer for holding our own little sports meetings, when track and field events were engaged in with the same enthusiasm as imbued our footballing efforts. One of the outstanding features of the Lewis summer season was the Stornoway Football League Sports in Willow Glen, which were in character rather like the Highland Games held on the mainland of Scotland, and we boys used the banks of the Laxdale river to emulate those more sophisticated activities.

Our time was not altogether confined to these strenuous games. Many hours were spent on the 'Cockle Ebb' when the tide was out. The sandflats there were teeming with cockles, and through the sands the seaward flow of the Laxdale river meandered lazily. Wandering barefoot on quiet evenings or Sunday afternoons we dug out the cockles, using one to open another, rinsed the opened cockles in the river and ate them raw.

Both the 'Cobb' (a typical Hebridean shorthand abbreviation for Cockle Ebb) and the river mouth are now so polluted that no one could possibly eat the cockles, or anything rinsed in the water of the river.

Another pursuit at the Cobb was stalking flounders. We spent hours in the channel made by the river on its way through the sands, edging carefully forward with feet splayed, heels close together, gazing into the water. When a flounder moved it left a little trail, and just before it came to rest it gave a sort of convulsive wriggle that raised a small cloud of sand. This sand settled on the fish, endorsing what was already being achieved by natural camouflage. Although the stalker saw no change of colour on the bottom, long experience enabled him to pick out the shape, and a slow quiet approach was made towards its nose. When the flounder moved again it very often went nose first into the 'v' between its pursuers heels. The feet were then brought together over the fish, and searching fingers found the gills for lifting it out of the water.

Sometimes a few big enough to take home were caught, but most were put back as too small. The thrill of the chase was the thing.

When the tide was flooding or ebbing we sometimes went swimming in the river channel, always with the tide, so that we could enjoy the sensation of moving past the bank faster than Olympic swimmers. Our speed through the water was very ordinary but the speed of the rushing waters over the ground made our progress look spectacular.

Our headmaster at Laxdale told us that when the Vikings named the place they did so because of how rich the river was in salmon. Alas, by the time I went to live there, and then in Newvalley, very few salmon tried to get up and of these not many reached the spawning beds. There were, however, sea trout and brown trout, affording another means of pleasure and relaxation. I spent many hours with a rod on the river, not catching much more than criticism for wasting my time when I should be studying.

More than fishing with the rod and line I enjoyed guddling. I would disturb the fish by thumping on the bank, and as the startled fish moved I watched where they went. I then waited patiently, giving them time to settle, before moving slowly and quietly into position, trying not to create any disturbing vibration of the bank. Lying prone on the bank the sleeve of my jersey would be rolled up to the shoulder, and the arm lowered silently into the water behind the fish. The hand was then brought into position over the tail and moved gently towards the gills (which were opening and closing rhythmically as the trout 'breathed') with the thumb on one side and the fingers on the other, just, but only just, touching the fish. Then, timing the movement of the hand to the movement of the gills, the thumb and fingers were inserted and with a flick of the wrist and a snatch of the elbow it was on the bank. I landed sea trout and brown trout by this method.

Guddling was truly a fascinating way of fishing. What started me off was going down by the river one Sunday evening in a state of utter frustration at the superstitious taboo (there were many others) on taking a fishing rod on Sunday. Then I remembered having heard of this method. The evening was fine, the river bank was dry for lying prone over a pool: I would try it, which I did with some success. From then on I was hooked.

I did not dare produce the two brown trout that I caught that first evening, so I put them in fresh water in a tub in the peat-shed, and produced them on Monday.

The castle grounds were a favourite haunt both winter and summer, with Willow Glen and the gorge of the Creed from its mouth to the Arnish bridge holding pride of place on about equal terms. Walking along the many winding and intricate paths in that wonderful place was an adventure in itself. But we didn't keep to the roads and pathways, and an action that started in Willow Glen could emerge on the Arnish Moor on the far side of the river Creed without a path being used except when crossing it.

My two most frequent companions on these scrambles were John Roderick (always referred to as John R.) Maclean and James (Soil) Graham. The war lost me another of my boyhood friends when James, who was in the RAF, was killed in action over Germany.

10

No trocair here

A NYONE READING THIS FAR might be excused for wondering whether, during these busy years, I ever went to school. I did – reluctantly. There was never a time when I would not have preferred to be doing something else; a preference that may be understood when one considers how many somethings else there were to be done in the realms of work and play.

Apart from the two years when I was taught by Miss Maclennan, whom I have mentioned before, I have little recollection of the elementary educational process as operating in the Laxdale Public School. With Miss Maclennan I developed a reasonable fluency in the use of English, although I was still plagued by my seemingly incorrigible lisp. It was with her guidance that I was conscious of the first stirrings of appreciation of English poetry. My father had made Gaelic poetry, in prose and verse, part of my life.

When a poetry lesson was over, if there was a 'picture' in the poem, we would be asked to do a pastel drawing of what we saw, or thought we saw; and on one of these occasions Wordsworth's daffodils, fluttering and dancing in the breeze beside the lake, appeared on the class drawing sheets in a variety of incredible guises.

In addition to fostering appreciation and understanding of language there seems to have been an emphasis on learning to communicate, and we were given many essays to write. The poetry reading, essay writing and drawing I enjoyed, probably explaining why I remember best those two years and that aspect of my elementary education. The other subjects in the curriculum were not neglected, however. We got the stipulated quota of arithmetic, history and geography, but these subjects did not make such an impression on me.

When we moved into the 'master's' room, again with the prospect of a two-year stint, the atmosphere was very different.

First of all the room itself, if my memory can be trusted, was to the north side of the building, and larger, darker and colder than the one we left. It was made clear to us at once that a harsh discipline held sway, based on the 'lion's tail' (which I have referred to before). At one end of the room there was a small blackboard at the top of which were chalked the letters NTH, and underneath, in brackets, the elucidation NO TROCAIR HERE – *trocair* being the Gaelic word for mercy. There followed a list of the offences for which there was no mercy, a list so comprehensive that he might as well have written NO TROCAIR – PERIOD.

The new conditions were ones to which most of us adapted and with which we learned to live in a state of watchful truce. Some rebels, however, who started on the wrong foot at loggerheads with the headmaster, were unable to come to terms with the situation and spent the two years waiting desperately for the day of escape.

In retrospect I would say that more time was spent on arithmetic than on all the other subjects together, although before the end of the second year (our last in elementary school) we were given an initiation into Latin, science, algebra and geometry.

Next in importance to arithmetic, or possibly before, came music; and he tried to make everyone join in, however disconcerting this might prove to be. During one singing session he suddenly realised that I was not participating. I wasn't because I have always been aware of some of my own more obvious limitations, and I knew that compared with the golden-throated warblers in the Laxdale Gaelic Choir any sounds that I produced would be like the cawing of a rook with laryngitis.

He stopped in front of me, and – not speaking so as not to interrupt the singing – he signalled to me to open my mouth. I didn't. He then tried to insert the end of the wooden pointer that he was using as a conductor's baton, between my front teeth with a levering movement to open them. He didn't. My mouth remained closed; and I never opened it again to try to sing a single note in the remaining two years at the school. I am convinced that it was only my flair for arithmetic, especially mental arithmetic for which he had a passion, that saved me from what could have been painful consequences.

Two chores that were performed by final-year boys were the pumping of water to the storage tank that supplied the schoolhouse, and the cleaning and inking of blackboards last thing on Friday afternoons in readiness for the next week's chalkings. For the pumping we took turns at working an unwieldy iron handle up and down until a spurt of water from an overflow pipe on the roof indicated a full tank.

The blackboard inking was generally accompanied by discreet horseplay, and apart from finishing the task with black hands, our bare knees, faces and clothes collected their quotas of ink. For this service there was compensation in the form of a payment of one penny each, made by the headmaster. When we were set at liberty for the weekend there was a rush to the nearest shop, where resources were pooled according to purchase requirements.

The smokers combined in twos, and the five Woodbines for two pence were shared out – two and a half cigarettes each. The scholars with a sweet tooth combined to buy and share Highland Cream toffee. I don't know what the cigarettes did to the lungs, but I do know that the toffee was of no lasting benefit to the teeth.

One duty that I performed with two or three other boys is in itself a social comment on the times of which I write. There was such a discrepancy between the prices charged for staple groceries in the town of Stornoway, and in fact throughout the whole island, and the prices in the south of Scotland, that salaried people who could do so made a very considerable saving by having large hampers of goods sent at regular intervals from food stores in Glasgow or Paisley. These (in our headmaster's case) we emptied, handing in the packages removed from the hamper for storing in the schoolhouse larder. Even at that age I think that I was aware of the implications of this inequitable set-up – that it was those of us who had least who paid most.

The opening of Lipton's shop created within one week a revolution in the grocery trade in the town of Stornoway. When the window blinds were raised on the first day of business startled shoppers stared in utter disbelief at the prices on the items displayed. So much so that some women were heard to express the opinion that there must be something wrong with goods being offered at such low prices.

Some initial suspicion soon disappeared as the shopping public discovered the quality of the goods being offered. In other shops, in most cases within a week, prices came tumbling down. Groceries were being purchased in a number of instances at less than half of what had been the standard price for years. For the first time the people realised to what extent the local merchants had held them up to ransom. The low paid, the unemployed, war pensioners, the old, all were now finding that the weekly pittance was going nearly twice as far as before.

There was one diversion that I instigated while in the 'master's' room that got a group of us into trouble. I cannot remember whether I had ever seen it done before (I think I must have) or whether I invented it. The idea was to find a pool in the river, not very deep, so situated that we could lie prone beside it with the hands set on two stones, a little wider than the shoulders, in such a way that the head could be lowered into the pool. A flat stone was placed on the bottom of the pool, and on the stone a pebble. The game was to take the pebble from the bottom in one's mouth.

It was playtime on a glorious summer's day the first time that we tried this game, becoming so absorbed that we were still at it when the bell rang. There was a concerted rush from the river, over the playground wall and across to the top gate leading to the school, because we knew that the headmaster would be in his usual place at the classroom door twirling the 'lion's tail', and that the last in would receive the customary lash on the bottom of his pants.

When we did get to our seats there were about half a dozen of us with dripping wet hair, and with trickles of water running down our faces and necks. He looked at us in irate wonder and asked for an explanation.

He was told quite simply and truthfully by one of our number: 'We were dipping our heads in the river, sir.' A signal for him to do a characteristic ritual war dance in front of us, flicking the 'lion's tail' with his fingers and bellowing: 'F for fools and F for floods.'

That was as far as he went, probably because there were so many of us, mostly his best pupils, involved. We were very careful not to try that pastime again during school hours.

11

The Nicolson

TIME PASSED. Our two years in the 'master's' room came to an end. The school closed for the summer holidays and the knowledge that I would not be returning brought no regrets, although there was some trepidation at the prospect of moving to a new school when the holidays were over.

For my secondary education I would be going to *sgoil a bhaile* (the town school), as the Nicolson Institute was called in the villages near the town. In Shawbost we had referred to it as *sgoil Steornabhaigh* (the Stornoway school). The various pursuits of the long summer kept the mind from dwelling on the bondage to come, but there were some black moments when thoughts of the unknown clouded the horizon. Having an older brother at the Nicolson Institute was a help as he tried to reassure and encourage me, nevertheless I thought of it as hostile territory, with the prospect of strange classmates, strange teachers and more than likely, strange new methods of teaching.

That same year there was a further addition to the Smith family – a son. He was named Donald John.

Donald, another of my father's brothers, who had been in the Merchant Navy where tuberculosis was then an occupational disease, had come home to die of that ailment. He was in the local sanatorium at the time (he died shortly afterwards), so the new baby was given his name. John was added for uncle John of the *Iolaire* disaster – probably the girl's name Johanna originally given was deemed inadequate.

On going to the Nicolson (it was rarely given its full title of Nicolson Institute by its pupils) I quickly got to know my teachers and made new friends. Besides, a number of my Laxdale classmates were there although none was in my class. There were also pupils from Laxdale on higher classes. Soon I was as much 'at home' in the Nicolson as I had been at Laxdale – at least as much at home as I would ever be in a school. I still didn't like it.

Nevertheless I entered upon my secondary education with some success. In those days it was customary, if a pupil obtained top marks in a subject in a term examination, to indicate this by placing an asterisk against that subject in the report sent to the parents. On my first term report there were five or six of these 'stars' – I cannot remember exactly how many. What I do remember is my father chuckling, 'Tha seo mar an grioglachan le reannagan' – 'This is like the Pleiades with stars.'

Before the end of the first year my name was put forward (I think by my teachers or the rector) for a competitive bursary examination. Top performance pupils from first, second and third year were eligible and I was delighted when in due course the rector announced at Monday morning assembly that I had won.

He had a clipped abrupt way of speaking and made my success sound like an indictable offence when he said, 'The Nicolson bursary competition has been won by a first-year pupil. A most unusual result – and an unusual pupil.' I was much more pleased by the £5 per annum that was the value of the bursary than by any prestige that might attach to the result.

That first year there were awkward as well as successful moments. One incident has remained in my mind, possibly because I could never tolerate injustice. After one of the term examinations we were given back our geometry papers and I had the very encouraging mark of 90 out of a possible 100. There were ten questions, and on checking back on where I had gone wrong I was quite sure, after a careful scrutiny, that I had answered correctly. It took me some time to find the courage to go out in front of the class and point this out to the teacher. She agreed that I had answered correctly and then said, 'Well: No examination paper is perfect, I'll give you 98 out of 100.'

I went back to my seat thinking, 'No one else in the class has answered all ten questions correctly, and no one else in the class has lost marks because of lack of perfection.' I must confess that it rankled. But I had already discovered from past experience that not all teachers were possessed of a clearly defined sense of justice.

It was that same year, this time in the geography class, that I again had occasion to question the marking of my examination papers. We were doing the geography of Ireland, and part of the examination consisted of entering certain mountain ranges, loughs, rivers and towns on a blank map. One of the rivers that had to be entered was the Blackwater, and I had noted that in addition to the main Blackwater river running into the sea to the south-east of Ireland there was another much smaller Blackwater river running westwards into Lough Neagh. So, having the kind of mind that latches on to such inconsequential but interesting bits of information, I had entered both on the map.

When the papers were returned to me there was a large red X against the entry showing the river running into Lough Neagh, and no mark at all against the other entry. I approached my teacher with the papers and some trepidation and pointing to the red X in the top right-hand corner of the map I said: 'Excuse me, sir, but you have marked that entry as wrong.'

'Ahumm' – he had a habit of prefacing his remarks with what sounded like a miniature throat-clearing exercise – 'Ahumm my boy. Yes I have. The Blackwater river is down there.' – thumping the bottom right-hand corner of the map with an admonitory index finger.

'Yes sir. I've put that one in.'

'Oh, I see. Very clever! You put it in two places hoping one of them was right.'

'No sir. I put it in two places because there are two Blackwater rivers.'

After one disbelieving look at me he grabbed the atlas, opened it at the map of Ireland, and then said: 'Ahumm, you're quite right my boy, quite right.' He promptly marked both entries as correct and adjusted my examination percentage accordingly.

Looking back, I cannot think that such incidents were calculated to make me a favourite with my teachers.

I remember the same teacher, I think he was correcting examination papers at the time, telling us to do some revision while he got on with what he was doing. It was an opportunity not to be missed. My copy of Herman Melville's *Moby Dick* came out, and my head went down. I was engrossed, quite oblivious of the teacher's approach when he decided to take a quiet look at what we were up to. I was jolted back from literary involvement to stark reality when he barked 'What do you think you're doing?'

'Reading, sir,' I said.

'And what are you reading?' he went on.

'*Moby Dick*, sir.'

'I'll *Moby Dick* you', he bellowed.

He didn't; he gave me an ear-shattering, open-handed smack to the side of the head that made me see more stars than ever appeared on my term reports. I was most incensed, in retrospect, about this attack when I discovered that for one of the third-year classes *Moby Dick* was prescribed reading.

On another occasion during an English lesson he asked for words beginning with auto 'as for example in automatic or automobile'.

We had by no means exhausted the more than fifty such words in the English language when I made the mistake of giving him 'auto-suggestion'. A mistake because the 'suggestion' part of it was extraordinarily difficult for a person with my type of lisp. In fact it was impossible. He said: 'Auto – what?'

I said 'Auto-suggestion, sir,' and adding the sir didn't improve the diction. He asked again, and I tried again, without success, but my obvious speech defect evoked no sympathy. Much to the amusement (at my expense) of the class, he kept on asking – until at last I spelt it out for him letter by letter. I was not amused; although it did occur to me to suggest a word of my own – 'autohellwithit'.

I think that it was the following year that I was quietly

coaxed on to the path to articulate speech. Strangely
enough no teacher had ever suggested that I should have
remedial treatment or speech training, and when the
advice did come it was from an unlikely source, a second
cousin of my own, Murdo Macaulay.

Murdo's grandfather (his mother's father) and my
grandfather (my father's father) had been brothers; and
family ties being as they are in Lewis, when the Macaulay
family moved from Bragar to Laxdale immediate contact
was made.

I called one evening, some time after they arrived, and
Murdo was in alone. If my memory serves me right he
was working at the Manor Farm at the time and had
spent the day ploughing.

Although not many years older than I, as there was no
one else present he took the opportunity to have a candid
talk with me and to give me advice that proved
invaluable. Roughly what he said to me was this:

> You are doing exceptionally well at school. If you
> keep it up a varied choice of careers will be open to
> you. But unless you do something about that lisp of
> yours it will be a hindrance all your life; and it will
> bar you from many pursuits as well as being an
> embarrassment. Your mother has told me that
> according to the doctor there is nothing wrong with
> your tongue, and it seems to me that you are taking
> your lisp for granted. Now, instead of accepting it,
> why don't you try to cure it? Train yourself to
> speak. Practise trying to say every word clearly.
> Work at it. When you are walking alone, with no
> one about, recite poetry to yourself, repeat bits and
> pieces you've learned by heart – the shorter
> catechism, the Bible, anything! But try to do it

distinctly. I am sure in my own mind that you can do it if you try.

I tried. And I did.

I followed his advice about reciting aloud while on lonely walks with such dedication that once as a group of younger boys passed me I heard one remarking 'That's Safety. He's mad.' Murdo Macaulay, the ploughboy who gave me some of the most helpful advice that I have had in a long lifetime, later went into the Merchant Navy, took his master mariner's ticket, and in the war won a well-earned Distinguished Service Cross.

He really must have impressed me, and also succeeded in persuading me of what could be achieved: because although some of the more callous of my school mates were still, even in my second year in the Secondary, repeating the occasional mocking word after me, yet I applied myself to such good effect that less than three years later, I was beginning to pick up the courage to speak at the school Debating Society meetings.

Those of us going in to the Nicolson daily from the outlying villages, especially those from poor homes, were handicapped from the very beginning. The pupils living in the town, and those from the more distant rural villages who were in lodgings in the town could, in wet weather, got to and from school in a reasonably dry condition, and could get back to their homes or digs for a prepared meal at lunch time. For the unfortunates walking from Sandwick or Melbost, from Coulregrein, Laxdale, Guershader, Newvalley or Benside things were very different. The tentative encroachment of socialism on the vested interests of capitalism had not yet provided such modern refinements as school transport and school canteens.

In the Hebridean winter the prevailing climatic conditions are wind and rain, with occasional sleet or snow. All too often we arrived in the classroom cold, wet and bedraggled, and in some cases ill clad and ill-nourished, to sit there while our clothes dried on us by evaporation, from body heat assisted by the school central-heating system.

At lunch time we went to the 'Cookery'. This was a corrugated iron shack where Miss Craig, a dedicated and inspired domestic science teacher, passed on some of her own expertise to aspiring pupils, with equipment and in conditions that by today's standards were primitive in the extreme.

Here we were provided with cupboard space, where we could cache a tin of cocoa, and a tin, jar or paper bag of sugar; provided also was boiling water for mixing the cocoa. The 'eats' varied as did the means in the homes, mine were invariably a couple of slices of bread and margarine, sometimes with crowdie or a bit of cheese, carried in the jacket pocket, and often wrapped in newspaper; a paper bag or a sheet of greaseproof paper was hard to come by. I detested the smell and taste of newsprint.

Occasionally I had a special sandwich. If we were having fried liver for tea I would save a bit, and then in the morning slice the cold liver very thinly and use the slices as a sandwich filling for my bread and margarine. As I left home at half past eight in the morning and didn't get back until about a quarter to five or five o'clock in the evening there was little danger of my being overweight.

These conditions were more or less standard for the six years that I was at the Nicolson, with one exception. About halfway through I developed such an intense dislike for cocoa that not only could I not drink the stuff any more; I didn't even want to go to the 'Cookery' where I could smell it. For about the last three years I ate my 'piece' outside, and washed it down with a drink of water from the tap – a 'deoch at the gock' in Stornoway parlance. The next time that I drank cocoa was on active service during the war, but that was navy 'kye' and was more a food than a drink!

These circumstances can scarcely be considered as encouraging scholastic endeavour; and in many instances conditions in the home were no better.

In my own case there was such gross overcrowding (ten and later eleven persons in two tiny rooms) and so many tasks had to be done that I could not find adequate space or tine for any worthwhile study. Reading could be done in any place where one could stand or sit. Something more was required for written work, and as a consequence this was restricted to essential nightly homework that must be done to avoid punishment. Working in winter at one end of a narrow table, by the light of a smoky paraffin lamp, I was glad to put away my exercise books as soon as the set work was completed.

Sometimes when the rain was very heavy a weather eye had to be kept out for the *sileadh* (drips of water seeping through the thatch). A drop of *sileadh* left a starry brown stain where it landed, and at all costs the virgin whiteness of exercise books must be protected from such violation.

I found that the best position for writing an essay was lying face down on the floor, and the best time immediately after some hard work. In spring, summer and autumn I would come in from croft or peats when an essay had to be written, and without a pause or rest take up my prone position with my exercise book. The ideas and words would then flow in sufficient quantity to pass muster with my English teacher. In winter, when I must begin an essay without the 'warming up' of physical action beforehand, I found writing much more difficult.

Not one of my teachers had any concept of the conditions in which I was living; nor thinking back, did any of my classmates. I have no recollection of any one of them being inside our house in all the years that I was at the Nicolson.

I should explain more fully what is meant by the word *sileadh* used here. When it rained the water seeped through the thatch of these houses, the soot of years dissolving in it and making it dark brown in colour. This process of dripping sooty water was known as *sileadh* and was quite a problem in almost every house during heavy rain, or a thaw after a heavy fall of snow. The placing of household utensils such as basins, bowls, jugs, pots and pans under the spot where the *sileadh* was worst, was usually quite inadequate – there was generally an insufficient number of these receptacles to go round – and if they were not watched and emptied they soon overflowed. Quite often only a half-hearted attempt was made to cope with this visitation. The result was that rivulets flowed along the clay floors and pools formed all over them. There was a philosophic kind of resignation about the attitude of the people to these minor troubles. One could not stop the rain, and anyway, it couldn't go on forever.

One story told was with a bearing on these conditions. In the days before bus services became widespread, the youths from the outlying districts of the Island, who were attending the secondary school at Stornoway, often went home for the weekend. They walked, of course. This practice was, however, frowned upon by many of the teachers, as the incentive to work while in the country for the weekend was not very great. In addition it required no very elaborate excuse to prevent some of these youths from turning up on Monday morning.

One particular Friday evening, however, several of them set out for their homes, despite constant warnings from the teacher. This band was particularly unfortunate; it started raining that same evening, and rained incessantly all through the weekend until late on Sunday night when the boys would have to tramp back to town. They were very disappointed as they had all looked forward to having a good time. But the teachers, of course, thought it had served them right for having gone home, and one of them couldn't conceal his Lucretian pleasure in the situation. He said rather ironically to one of the youths concerned, 'Well, well! I suppose you had a very good weekend yourself, especially with the *sileadh*.'

'Oh yes!' came the reply, 'I had a most enjoyable time. I spent the whole weekend sitting on a table dangling my legs, with a treacle-scone on a piece of string, fishing in the *sileadh* for my grandmother.'

This was an exaggerated tale, to cope with a rather difficult and exasperating situation, but the very fact that such a tale was even thought of will give you an idea of how this *sileadh* was a very real thing in the lives of the people.

12

'Round Achmore':
Stornoway and after

IN THE RURAL COMMUNITIES of Lewis there were three persons in the Godhead: the minister, the doctor and the schoolmaster, a trinity that was treated by the crofting population with a deference approaching that accorded to the deity. It was inevitable as a consequence that the crofter saw one of these professions as the ultimate goal for any child who made the grade in higher education. And within the education system itself a greater emphasis was given to 'academic' subjects as being the means by which these goals could be attained. Only the rare exception opted out of the main stream and went in pursuit of eccentric careers like law, pharmacy or engineering!

During my first year at the Nicolson I had taken top marks in art (drawing) and handwork (woodwork) in each of the three term examinations. I was also taking Gaelic as one of my first-year subjects, but the curriculum set-up for second year was such that I could not take both art and Gaelic. So I was sent for by the rector who advised me to drop art as it was a subject that would not in the future be of any use or benefit to me. This was advice that I accepted with regret as I enjoyed the art class.

In my second year I took top marks in Gaelic two terms out of three and at the end of that year the rector sent for me again. This time he advised me to drop Gaelic and take Greek in third year. He told me that I already knew all the Gaelic that I was ever likely to require. At the time I had no very clear idea of what I wanted to do, and was naive enough to think that he knew what was best for me better than I did, so I agreed.

At the end of one year of Greek, for which I developed a distaste that verged on being a phobia, the rector didn't send for me: I went to see him and I told him, leaving no room for argument, that I would not be continuing with Greek in fourth year.

Sometimes I have wondered what he would have said if I had told him at the end of first year (with my good results in drawing and woodwork) that I wanted to be a joiner. Anyway, I didn't think of it. Like everyone else I had been conditioned into thinking in terms of academic success.

This was the era of the 'Intermediate Certificate', and mine didn't list art, Gaelic or Greek, as I had only one year of each subject. The certificate was worthless anyway.

From the beginning of the fourth year onwards my work at school, apart from English, deteriorated beyond recognition; and my term examination results were only a little better than average. This may have been the end result of several contributory factors – the amount of work I did outside school, the conditions of over-crowding at home, and more than likely the way I had been 'buggered about' in my first three years. I just seemed to lose interest.

The English class was quite different. At the beginning of my third year I found myself in the class being taken by Norman B. Anderson, and had the inestimable good fortune to be one of his pupils for four years. It was a privilege for which I have been grateful all my life.

One of the anomalies of the curriculum that I have never been able to understand is why it should have been compulsory for me to take music (for which I had no aptitude) for all of the six years that I was at secondary school, and yet I couldn't take art, for which I had an obvious flair.

Even if the curriculum that I followed after first year had prevented the study of art with a view to taking a 'higher' qualification, surely some periods of the week's timetable could have been devoted to it.

For the most part school life was dull to the point of being dreary, but there was no abatement of extramural activities. There were the morning and afternoon intervals or playtimes which were taken up with the usual romps and games; and for those of us who took 'pack lunches' the hour break in the middle of the day presented an opportunity not to be wasted. Without rushing things, lunch such as it was could be disposed of in about ten minutes, leaving us still hungry but also leaving us with fifty minutes of free time before returning to incarceration in the classroom.

A group of four or five of us were often together, and in a town like Stornoway it was inevitable that we should spend a deal of time in the harbour area. There something was always happening: cargo boats discharging coal, bricks, cement, timber, slates, grain, consumer goods, the merchandise being imported for the whole island; fishing boats, depending on the season, discharging herrings or white fish; the herrings being soused with salt as the baskets were emptied into wooden 'kits'; the white fish, halibut, ling, cod, coal fish, skate, all laid out in rows to await buyers gathering in response to the salesman's hand-bell. I found all the activity fascinating, as did my companions.

We sometimes deserted the quays for the town, and would stand outside a blacksmith's shop watching a horse being shod, or a length of white-hot iron being shaped on the anvil; or stand at a building site where masons and bricklayers were using their skills.

When the building of the Stornoway Town Hall began we got some real scope for our work-watching; one operation that we found engrossing was the shaping and carving of the sandstone facings being done by the hewers. They worked in long open-fronted shelters, and day after day we made a point of spending some time observing them at work. One of the hewers was a John Maclean who lived quite near to me in Newvalley, and on whom, quite naturally, I focused much of my attention. He was a skilled, painstaking craftsman, who took a pride in his work; nevertheless, he always had time for a word with me.

About a quarter of a century later Carn House, on South Beach in Stornoway, against one end of which was built the Town Hall, was demolished. As a result of the demolition an unfinished part of the Town Hall wall equivalent in area to the gable-end of Carn House had to be reinstated.

A sufficient quantity of the red Isle Martin stone required for the work was available in the burgh yard: this had been salvaged over the years from demolition work throughout the town and hoarded for possible future use. The only question was, who would do the reinstatement? When this was raised in the Town Council, of which I was a member at the time, I suggested John Maclean; he came out of retirement to oblige us.

I stopped one day to have a word with him and to admire his handiwork (as I had done as a boy), and it was then that he told me that he had worked as an apprentice at the building of the original Town Hall (it was destroyed by fire shortly after the First World War), that he had worked as a journeyman bricklayer and hewer at the building of the present Town Hall, and here he was now, still active, doing this reinstatement.

When the job was completed it gave me great pleasure to move that an appreciation of his work be minuted by the council, and this was done.

One conclusion I came to from my many hours of watching men at work is that all really skilful work – whether done by a labourer wielding a brush, shovel, spade or pick, or whether done by a master craftsman wielding the tools of his trade – is based on rhythm and the economy of movement and of effort that goes with it. That is why a man who is good at his work makes it look easy.

Some time ago a commercial traveller, with a short time to spare from business while in Stornoway, asked to be taken for a short 'spin' in a motor-car, that he might see something of the Island. He was taken 'round Achmore'.

On his return to town he was asked what he had seen, and replied, rather disgustedly: 'Miles and miles and miles of bugger all.' This man may not have been blind, but it is difficult to believe that he was not very short-sighted. There were many things to see, and quite a few tales to be told of that little journey.

Here, however, the driver may have been at fault: perhaps he didn't even think of telling stories about places which they passed on the way. If he had, the traveller might not have been so obviously bored. He should have heard something, however little, even if he saw only 'miles of bugger all'.

On this route there is that very picturesque, if unbeautiful, settlement, scattered with such little regard for rhyme or reason on the hillocks among and around the bogs of Marybank. People now have stopped wondering why of all the places conveniently near the town of Stornoway, this watery desert should have been chosen for permanent settlement by one-time nomads, and others. In such a question a stranger, however, might find food for thought.

Possibly these settlers were as long-headed as the men of the road have a reputation for being. They may have foreseen the requisitioning of land round about the town by the county council for housing schemes, and by the Stornoway Trust for the settlement of smallholders. If so, it was patent that this particular stretch of roadside bogland where they pitched their tents and built their huts could never be used for such purposes. Here no economic excuse could be put forward for eviction. So here they came, and it looks very much as if they had all come to stay.

In the evenings, when the shadows have softened down harsh outlines and the reddish lights of oil-lamps from the windows are reflected in the bogs and pools, when the stars are shining in the sky behind, when the passerby wonders whether he is looking at the silhouette of an unlit hut, or a peat-stack, at wireless aerials or at clothes lines, it is something not to be missed. And sometimes the passerby will stop to listen to the skirl of the pipes, the music of an accordion or mouth-organ, the screeching of a too-often played gramophone record, or the BBC accents of a news commentator, coming across the peat-banks from this strange place where everybody seems to be so unexplainably happy.

Then out by the Peat Farm, where the only things produced without excessive and backbreaking labour are peat, bog and water; and so by little lochs and hills, by sheilings on green hillocks, and by stretches of brown moorland to the Ghost Rock.

Here above the road is a beautiful loch, surrounded by hills and rocks, from which flows a boulder-strewn burn trickling under the road and winding down to another loch on the level stretch of moor below. Just past the burn, rising above the road and slightly overhanging a little green, is the Ghost Rock – haunted since times long forgotten by what particular ghost, no one seems to remember.

Passing the place on a moonlit night, a young man, fortified by the presence of his lady-friend, decided it might be amusing to find out her reactions to the mention of the ghost. Had he been alone, probably he would have walked past very quickly looking straight ahead and taking good care not to see the dark shadows under the rock.

On this particular night the shadow under the rock was occupied by a man asleep. He had been in Stornoway and as was and still is the custom with the majority of country dwellers in Lewis when they visit the town, he had drunk much more than was good for him. To walk home in this condition had been beyond him and, unfortunately, it was under the Ghost Rock that his strength failed. Here he slumped down on the grass and stayed in a drunken stupor.

The young man, while passing with the lady, feeling quite uncertain himself as to whether he believed in spirits or no, suddenly clutched his companion's shoulder and exclaimed, 'Take her, Ghost!'

From the dark shadows beside the road came a strange voice, thick with sleep and drink – 'Give her to me.'

The sleeper had just awakened; it is recorded that the young man easily won the race to the top of the Ghost Rock brae.

On for another half mile and in front can be seen the outer end of the village of Leurbost, beyond rise the hills of Lochs and Harris, and then turning right along the Cleascro road, the blue domes and peaks of the Uig Hills are seen in the distance. Here, on the very rocky slopes of a hill, you pass what is left of one of the few plantations of trees in Lewis apart from those around the town. They are windswept, gnarled, twisted and broken, looking as if some giant had kicked his way through them.

From there the road continues by little lochs and hills through the village of Cleascro, by the inner end of Achmore and then by more sheilings, lochs, hills and streams on the way back to town.

When passing over the River Creed, remember the story of the man who chased the 'ghosts', at this bridge, into the moors. Where every village had its own ghost or ghosts, it is perhaps not strange that a very prevalent idea of a good practical joke should be to frighten people at night. But on this occasion, as on many others, the haunting was not very successful from the point of view of the 'ghosts'.

There was one man, well known for his nerve and strength, who had a reputation for fearing neither man nor devil and he used this road at any and every hour of the night, to and from Stornoway. On one occasion several young men from Achmore decided to test Angus' courage by waylaying him and doing a 'ghost act'. They chose the Creed bridge for their rendezvous and all of them, as they saw their victim's unmistakable swing in the distance, hid under the bridge with the exception of one of their number who, draped in a white sheet, stood swaying eerily in the middle of the roadway.

Strange and unearthly moans rose from the river; the ghostly white figure in the roadway swayed and flapped; the man came on. The moans were varied with ghostly shrieks, and the white ghost stood still. The man was only a few yards away now and knowing his great strength the 'ghost' was beginning to become worried.

And then, when almost stepping on to the bridge, without slackening his pace, Angus addressed the wraith: 'Well, stranger, if you're a human being it is high time you took to your heels, but if you're the devil I'm afraid there isn't much good of even my tackling you!'

With a flurry of white sheet the would-be ghost tore along the road and then across the moor to be followed closely by the scrambling 'noises off' from under the bridge. They were satisfied now about the truth of Angus' reputation; he, for his part, went on his way chuckling.

There is another little tale told about Angus which gives one an idea of the type of man he was. Walking in Bayhead in Stornoway one day, he was surprised to see a bull ambling down the street; two men followed in the distance gesticulating wildly and obviously exhorting the population to clear out of the way. They required little encouragement! Men and women were dashing in all directions, while Angus walked calmly on.

Then, just as the bull was passing he leapt, and, timing his spring amazingly for one of his massive proportions, clutched a horn in each hand. A heave of his mighty shoulders and a wrench, and he held the animal until its pursuers came up with the rope.

One of the men, who knew him, said, 'Man Angus, you had an awful nerve tackling a bull!' 'Huh,' came the response contemptuously from Angus. 'What's a bull anyway, but a grown up calf!'

The Creed bridge is left far behind and listening to these tales will take the traveller a little on his way.

In by Loch Airidh na Lice – always worth seeing – lying in the valley between two hills, by Maryhill, the old water-works, the war memorial, and so along the north wall of the castle grounds, back to Stornoway, you have gone the road of 'miles and miles of bugger all!' You have gone the route that has always been known in Stornoway as going 'round Achmore'.

Duppie

On release from school at the end of the day the time taken to get home to Newvalley could vary greatly, depending on many factors. If some urgent task had to be done, as happened frequently, the way home was down Matheson Road, out the sanatorium road, across the stile park and through Guershader. Should there be no urgency we might go round by the harbour, or through the town, or through the castle grounds, or out by Laxdale – the route depending on who were in the group that day and what diversion we had in mind. As I mentioned before one of my regular tasks on getting home was going for a barrow of peats; a recurring chore that prevented my participation in many escapades.

Shortly after I went to the town school Donald

(Duppie) MacKenzie, who lived in a cottage he had built on the common pasture in the Cnoc Mor, had asked me to pick up the daily paper for him at the newsagent's in Stornoway. I was going into the town anyway, and it would save him a special trip each day. Once a week I picked up *The Topical Times* a small weekly publication taken up entirely with sport, if I remember correctly, and with quite a bit of space devoted to boxing; a sport in which Donald was intensely interested. He had boxed as a featherweight with the Seaforth Highlanders in India, and he had also done some long-distance running and had won the two-mile race at the British Army Sports at Lucknow – I think it was in 1908.

He was soon giving me boxing lessons; and just watching the way he moved was an education. He had the grace and rhythm of a ballet dancer, with none of the flamboyance, and an energy-conserving economy of movement. I would lead with a straight left for his chin and my glove would pass harmlessly by the side of his head, which he had slipped to one side the three or four inches (never more than was necessary) to avoid the punch.

One evening he produced a cardboard box containing a set of boxing gloves – his own set – and he made me a present of them. I was as pleased as if I had won an Olympic medal. These gloves were in my possession for many years and quite a number of boys were introduced to the 'noble art' while wearing them.

Using a peat-iron, a pick or a spade, whatever he did requiring physical effort, Donald's every movement was easy and elegant. In all the thirty years and more that I knew him I don't think I ever saw him make a jerky or clumsy movement.

Apart from our enthusiasm for sport Donald was also

interested in current affairs, and events at national and local government level came in for scrutiny and comment. In winter when delivering the paper after school we made arrangements for my evening visits, which were frequent. When we had exhausted sport and current affairs Donald would sometimes reminisce on incidents in an eventful life. In the first decade of the twentieth century he had seen action with the Seaforth Highlanders on the north-west Frontier of India. The Punjab, Baluchistan, Afghanistan, the Khyber Pass, Lahore, Peshawar, Karachi, Delhi, Kabul, Sikhs, Afghans, Pathans and Punjabis were all names of places and people that recurred in his tales of army life in India under the British Raj.

The Islanders, you see, went all over the world: mostly as merchant seamen, but also as soldiers. They went as emigrants too, and at the time of the Clearances as displaced persons. As a consequence, those at home had a worldwide perspective. From Timsgarry to Timbuktu, form Shader to Shanghai, far and wide were the place-names that were in familiar use at the little village ceilidhs. A seaman home on leave would tell of the local person whom he had seen in Buenos Aires; a soldier would tell of a friend he had met in Peshawar. The Islanders were everywhere.

In 1756, when Suraj ed-Daula incarcerated 146 British soldiers in a noisome place about twenty feet sqaure, with only one small window for ventilation, only twenty-three survived; this episode became known as the Black Hole of Calcutta.

Of these twenty-three survivors one was from the Island of Lewis. His family lived on a croft at 25 Eoropie, a little village in the Ness district. As I keep on repeating – you find and found the islanders everywhere.

After Donald had completed his term as a regular soldier he emigrated to Canada where he worked at different labouring jobs, supplementing his labourer's wage by boxing exhibition bouts.

His appearance as well as his skill was an attraction: he was so covered with picturesque tattoos that from the waist up he looked as if he were wearing an intricately designed skin-tight shirt, and his legs looked as if clad in tights to match. A working mate of his who was at one of these exhibition bouts told him afterwards that he had heard a spectator remark: 'If I was that guy I wouldn't work; I'd go on the stage full time.' Donald was highly amused.

He had acquired his extensive tattoos while with the army in India and he always maintained that it was because of an immunity stemming from this tattooing that he had never succumbed to any kind of fever in all his years of foreign service.

When war broke out in 1914 he returned from Canada with other Seaforth Reservists and saw action on the Western Front until taken prisoner in 1917. He was one of the handful (between thirty and forty I think) of his company that survived the hellish carnage on the Somme on 1 July 1916.

Sitting by a fine peat-fire on a winter's night he would slip occasionally into talk of those terrible times of mindless attrition – of the comrades who were gone.

There was the man who could throw a hand grenade further and more accurately than anyone in the battalion. Donald mentioned him many times; I suppose it was because of the respect of one athlete for another. This man had been killed in action. And there was the man who came to speak to Donald himself, before going down the line to go on leave, shook hands with him, wished him luck, and told him that he wouldn't be coming back to the trenches. He had come to the conclusion, he said, that they were engaged on a mad enterprise, supposedly sane civilised men killing each other indiscriminately to achieve nothing that would not in the end have to be decided at a conference table. He was not prepared to be involved any longer in such madness, and he even told Donald what he was going to do – he knew what English port to go to, where to get civilian clothes, how and where to get a berth on a merchant ship, in fact how to disappear without trace as far as his identity as a serving soldier was concerned.

Disappear without trace he did, until after a lapse of more than twenty years he got in touch with his next-of-kin in Lewis from the Antipodes. Curiously enough Donald didn't seem to think of him as a deserter, and never at any time questioned his courage; rather he seemed to admire him for backing up his principles with action.

But Western Front action for Donald himself ended when he was taken prisoner in 1917 while on night patrol. They were returning from the German lines with a prisoner for identification and questioning when they themselves were surrounded by a German patrol. The prisoner they had taken that night, and who was released when they themselves were captured, was a coporal of a Bavarian regiment, and he sustained a slight bayonet wound, inflicted accidentally by his lurching on the uneven ground on to the bayonet point of one of the patrol. After Hitler came to power in 1933 and Donald learned that he had been a corporal in the Bavarians, and had sustained a slight bayonet wound at the Western Front, he often speculated on whether it might have been Hitler whom he had held at bayonet point that night. So it was a prisoner-of-war camp for Donald Mackenzie, but it couldn't hold him. He escaped at his third attempt, just shortly before the war ended.

Each time he was recaptured he was moved to another camp, and he suffered much privation as a consequence of his efforts to escape; of course with the whole of Germany virtually starving at that stage in the war the prisoners' rations were frugal indeed. Until the end of his days it incensed him to see even a crust of bread being thrown away. When eating out of doors, as we did so often in the Hebrides, some thoughtless person would crumble a crust or remnant of food in the wrapping paper and throw it away. Donald would blast them: 'Put it out for the birds, give it to a sheep, take it home to the hens. Somewhere there is some one of God's creatures that will eat it. But DON'T throw it away!'

He told me the stories of his three escape attempts, and there was one incident in particular that impressed him very much. On his second attempt he had been on the run for six days. He had been travelling by night and lying up during the day. He had run out of food, in fact he hadn't eaten for two days, but he thought from the compass bearing he had been following and from the mileage that he reckoned he had covered that he was very close to the Dutch frontier. He was hiding in a clump of trees and an open space separated him from what he thought was a frontier track. The night was clear, with more light than he cared for, but he decided to risk it. He was more than halfway across the open space when the order to halt was barked from in front of him. He immediately let himself fall face down on the ground and remained perfectly still. Two German soldiers (they turned out to be frontier guards) came up, one on either side of him, with rifles at the ready. 'Escaped prisoner?' rapped one in English.

'Yes,' said Donald.

'Get up,' said the German.

Donald got up and they marched him to the frontier post.

Inside their hut he was asked how long he had been on the run. He told them six days, and he was then asked when he had last eaten. He told them he hadn't eaten for two days. Then the English-speaking German went to a shelf, picked up a metal box, opened it and handed it to Donald saying: 'All right, you eat those sandwiches'. Donald said: 'What about yourself? I'll take half of them, and thanks.'

'No,' said the German. 'You take them all. I'll share his,' pointing to his mate. Donald accepted gratefully.

'You are an Englishman?' said the German then.

'No! I'm a Scotsman' said Donald.

'What's the difference?' said the guard with a sardonic grin, 'Britannia rules the waves!'

'Who do you think is going to win the war?' he then asked.

'We are, without any doubt,' said Donald.

'Well,' said the guard, 'the allies may win the war, but I will tell you who is going to lose it – and that is the ordinary people of Germany, Britain, France, and all the other countries involved. Every war is lost by the ordinary people on both sides.'

When Donald was picked up for escorting back to prison the following morning his captors of the previous night wished him good luck, telling him that he had almost made it, and that it was a pity he had to be caught so close to freedom.

He did, however, make it on his next and third attempt.

When talking of being recaptured at the frontier one

109

could sense that even after so many years he still had a friendly feeling for that kindly German guard who gave his sandwiches to a hungry prisoner. In fact I am sure that he had more in common with him than he had with some of his neighbours in the Cnoc Mor!

On these evenings by the peat-fire in Donald's little cottage, his wife Isabella would make tea and set the table. The talk would go on as we partook of the excellent country fare always provided – eggs, crowdie, cheese, oatcakes, girdle scones, butter, jam and a copious supply of tea.

And when the evening was over Donald would accompany me part of the way home as if reluctant that the talk should end. In winter he made a point of having a good torch to light the way to the main road.

They treated me right royally at all times, and when twenty years later, as a town councillor and magistrate of the Burgh of Stornoway, I still visited them regularly they extended to me the same consideration, courtesy and kindness as they had done when I was a teenage schoolboy fetching the daily paper.

Politics

For me life in Newvalley was very much an out-of-school affair, and as I got older an additional interest was added to the number in which I was already involved. I was beginning to discover some of the implications of national politics.

The Hebrideans were always radical in their views. When the Highlands of Scotland were Conservative the Hebrides were Liberal. When Liberal ideas took over in the Highlands from Conservatism the Hebrides became socialist; the ideas from Conservatism to Liberalism were not so much 'new' as progressive. While canvassing and sometimes confronting opposing political ideas, the confrontation was rather courteous disagreement and good-natured banter than hostility.

As I have said before my father was a dedicated socialist, and my older brother John was now a member of the local constituency party. It is not surprising that I too became interested. There was a goodly band of socialist propagandists operating in and around Stornoway at that time. Names that spring to mind immediately are John Macaskill, Garden Road; Kenneth Macdonald, Sandwick; Donald Macleod, Knock; Murdo Montgomery, Laxdale; Roderick (Wedger) Mackay, Newvalley; John Kennedy, Stornoway; Margaret Macleod, Aird-a-Bhaigh; William Mackenzie, Dockers' Union; my father, and my brother John.

The political gospel was being spread in many different ways. A deal of useful work was done by prospective Labour candidates going round the constituency from door to door and talking to people in their homes. I myself had no experience of canvassing, but later on my role would be that of a speaker at pre-arranged and advertised public meetings, supporting the candidate and socialist policies.

During midday meal-breaks at work the believers were busy converting their fellow workers; and there were always opportunities for their kind of propaganda because if there is one thing that a Lewisman enjoys more than a good-going argument it is a continuation of the argument.

The Glasgow *Forward* was to Scottish socialism in the 1920s and 1930s what *Tribune* became after the last war to socialism throughout the country. The editor was Tom Johnston, who later, as Secretary of State for Scotland, laid the foundations of the North of Scotland Hydro Electric Board and became the board's first (unpaid) chairman. He was completely committed to the idea of harnessing the water power of the Highlands to generate energy for industrial and domestic use, and he used the *Forward* as a medium for propagating these ideas. But it took him a long time to get them implemented.

Perhaps it is just as well that he didn't live to see his idealistic concept become over-centralised, administratively top heavy and run by people who do not believe in socialism or nationalisation, and who have as much feeling for the Highlands and Islands as for the dark side of the moon.

But this is a digression. The founder father of the Hydro Board as editor of *Forward* attracted a galaxy of outstanding contributors to that great little weekly. Bernard Shaw, H. G. Wells, Cunningham Grahame, Beatrice and Sidney Webb, Arthur Greenwood, Ramsay Macdonald, James Barr, Macneill Weir, Joe Corrie (the miner poet and playwright), to name but a few, provided weekend reading for the workers and the unemployed of Stornoway and its outlying villages.

As a schoolboy I was roped in by Roddy (Wedger) Mackay, who lived two doors away from us in Newvalley, to distribute copies of *Forward* to the faithful in Laxdale and Benside on Saturday nights; it was read also in Sandwick and Melbost.

The effectiveness of the pioneer work going on – in the homes (candidates canvassing), at street corners (the unemployed), in trade-union offices (tradesmen, dockers and labourers at union meetings on Saturday afternoons or evenings), in huts and shelters on working sites (the workers having their midday meal-breaks), by readers of *Forward* (spreading the 'word' among neighbours), at

Labour Party meetings (by discussion and exchange of views), at public meetings (when politicians of national repute came to Lewis to speak) – is confirmed by the voting statistics. In the election of 1918 Labour polled 809 votes in the Western Isles constituency and in 1929 (the year of the flapper vote, when women first exercised the franchise) Labour's share was 5589, almost four and a half times as many.

Just how effective even the most modest medium of persuasion can be was brought home very clearly to me many years later – it was in fact in August 1970. I was standing in the railway station at Dingwall waiting for the morning train to Kyle of Lochalsh, which was running late as it was waiting at Inverness for the train from the south, when an official appeared and announced that the train had just left Inverness.

About five minutes later an old railwayman, who was standing at the edge of the platform, called out, 'Kyle train!' and I thought: 'It can't be! It only left Inverness five minutes ago.' Of course it wasn't; it was an engine doing some shunting manoeuvre at the siding outside the station.

There were a few ribald comments and laughs from the railwaymen who were standing by, and one made some remark – critical of British Rail – to which I hadn't paid much attention, with the obvious intention of stirring up a political reaction, when his mate, a man Macdonald whom I knew said, 'You needn't try to start an argument with this fellow [meaning me]. He's as much of a socialist as you are.' He had seen me at Labour Party meetings in Dingwall, 'Yes.' I said 'I've been a socialist since I was a schoolboy.'

'Well,' said Macdonald, 'I learned my socialism from little Red Murdo from Goathill, sitting in the hut during

113

the midday meal-break when I was working at housing schemes in Stornoway.'

I thought: 'That must have been my father,' but I wanted to be sure, so I said 'What work did you do?'

'I was a plasterer, and this man was a labourer with us. Every dinner hour he would get a discussion or an argument going. He had one son a schoolteacher, and another son at university. He had a big family and although only a labourer he was determined that they would all get the chance of a good education. We called him little Red Murdigie, and he was the man who taught me my socialism.'

I then said, 'You were a plasterer with Bert Macdonald – the Macdonald brothers, the plasterers from Muir-of-Ord?'

He looked surprised. 'Yes.' 'How did you know that?'

'Because', and I felt very proud as I said it, 'little Red Murdigie from Goathill, the labourer who taught you socialism, was my father.' I should point out here that the 'Red' in 'Red Murdo' referred to the colour of his ginger hair, not to his politics.

On another occasion – it was in 1954 in Stornoway – a ganger on one of the building sites came to speak to me when I was passing one day. He was from Point and said, 'You're a son of Murchadh 'an Fhionnlaigh?'

'Yes, I am,' I said.

'How is he keeping?'

'Oh, he's keeping very well, thank you.'

'Is he still arguing and talking socialism?'

'Yes, and he will be as long as he has breath with which to talk.'

'Well,' he said 'I worked with him at different building sites over the years, and I have never yet heard anyone set out an argument or state a case like your father.'

When I was on the Stornoway Town Council an old friend stopped me one day saying, 'Hold on a minute, Calum. You'll enjoy this, I was talking to your father the other day and I said to him: "That boy of yours that's on the Council – he's pretty good at making out a case when he's trying to get something done." And do you know what he said? – "Ma 'se dh-fhaodas. Nach do dh-ionnsaich mi fhein e!" – "So he should. Didn't I teach him myself!"'

One evening, it was either at the beginning of 1935 or at the end of 1934, my father came home from one of his meetings and told me that he had been instructed to ask me whether I would be interested in becoming prospective Labour candidate for the Western Isles.

My initial reaction was to treat the question as a joke, but when I was persuaded that he was serious I declined to have anything to do with the suggestion. Obviously I had no personal political ambitions, although for the life of me – now more than forty-five-years later – I have no idea what my motives were for saying no.

In 1935 Malcolm Kenneth Macmillan was chosen as candidate. He was a 22-year-old law student at Edinburgh University at the time, and in the general election the same year he became the MP for the Western Isles. When the results were announced he was carried shoulder-high by his jubilant supporters; it was a most appropriate gesture, because it was on the shoulders of these same pioneers who carried him then that he had climbed into Parliament.

Although I had been helping during the holidays in the campaign leading up to the election I was back at Glasgow University when the results were declared. Needless to say I was delighted; it was a victory for the sheer plodding dedication of devoted enthusiasts working over the years on a shoestring budget.

But all that was a long way into the future.

Bits and pieces

In May 1928, just before I was sixteen, I was offered my first trial game for the school First Eleven football team. It was an invitation that I had to decline because, either the previous night or in the early hours of that morning, there had been another (and this time a final) addition to the Smith family, and my mother had said to me that I should get back home from school as quickly as possible as the peat supply was getting very low and I must fetch a couple of barrow loads from the Cnoc Mor!

The team organisers, knowing how keen I was, just could not understand why I should turn down such an opportunity on the flimsy excuse that I had to go straight back home from school! But there was no resentment on my part; such an important family occasion superseded any personal considerations. The new arrival, another boy – there were now six sons and three daughters – was named Donald Murdo.

Apparently my grandfather Angus Macleod – Aonghas Dhomhnuill 'c 'urchaidh, my mother's father – had once expressed regret to my father that he had been unable to carry on his own father's or grandfather's names, Donald and Murdo, and my father had said to him that if things worked out right he would see to it that they were not forgotten. Now he was standing by something that he had half promised about twenty years earlier.

The tradition of carrying forward family names created some strange situations at times, and it was quite common to find two or sometimes even three persons with the same Christian name in one family, and then to be further confused by discovering that the father had the same name as well!

We now had two Johns – John and Donald John; two Murdos – Kenneth Murdo and Donald Murdo; and two Donalds – Donald John and Donald Murdo; but as they were all named after different people that made it all right.

Incidentally, although I missed an initial First Eleven game for the school because of D. M.'s arrival I played in the same half line with him for the Stornoway Athletic (he was centre half and I was right half) eighteen years later in 1946 after I came home from the war.

In between I had played for the school, Unionists, Sandwick, Caledonia, Rovers and in the navy for my ship and naval division.

As I got older I became more and more interested in games and sport, and I got a great deal of encouragement in Newvalley. I have already mentioned Donald (Duppie) Mackenzie, who gave me a set of boxing gloves. He also gave me a deal of useful advice on long-distance running – training and tactics. And living only two doors away from me was the incomparable Roderick (Wedger) Mackay.

I have mentioned him already in connection with socialist activities; but he was also very active in the local world of sports and football. He probably did more than any other single individual in the twenty years between 1919 and 1939 to encourage and maintain the Stornoway Football League Sports.

These were always held in the beautiful setting of Willow Glen; and Wedger, apart from administrative work, would spend many laborious hours with a team of helpers, cutting grass, preparing the running track and jumping pits, erecting roped-off barriers, putting up dressing tents, gathering the many bits and pieces of equipment required for such a day's activities – in fact performing a multitude of tasks without which such a meeting would be impossible.

On the day itself he would be there not only officiating but participating, and he was still performing many years after ordinary mortals would have given up and confined their activities to the sidelines.

I saw him when in his late forties, tossing a caber off which a length had to be cut before any of the other younger, heavier, bigger competitors could cope with it. And in his fiftieth year I saw him tying for first place in the pole-vault – the British Army record for which he had once held before the 1914–18 war. He also coached pole-vaulters and prospective heavy-event competitors.

D. D. (Hilton) Morrison, who monopolised first place in the pole-vault after Wedger stopped competing, was one of his protégés, and I remember Alec Urquhart (the Banker) and Donald (Chicky) Thompson getting lessons in tossing the caber, putting the shot, throwing the 56-pound weight, and Cumberland style wrestling, behind his house in Newvalley. As an absorbed observer I picked up a few tips that became quite useful later on, if only to pass on to others. I was much too light (about 10 stone 5 or 6 pounds) for such activities.

In retrospect what strikes me most about my last three years at secondary school is how little impression they appear to have made on me, at least as far as remembering events is concerned, as compared with what went on outside school life.

There were light-hearted moments, but my recollection is of putting up rather dourly with a situation that was not much to my liking. And strangely enough although I may have rebelled occasionally against school discipline it never occurred to me to rebel against the family discipline that insisted on my continuing with my formal studies.

On a number of occasions, when the going became intolerable, I went rambling in the castle grounds instead of going to school. Nor do I think that I have suffered any permanent damage from these truancies into an environment that I found much more rewarding than studying algebraic symbols or Latin grammar.

I remember one beautiful summer afternoon. My partner in the crime of dodging classes that day was Dolly (Brand) Maclean. When we reached the mouth of the Creed the tide was right for clambering over the rocks on to the island in the river mouth, so we made our way to the seaward side of the island, which was also the sunny side. After basking there for a while we decided to go for a swim and spent the hours, that would have been so boring had we been in classes, splashing about in the brine and then drying off in the sun.

I don't recollect ever playing truant by myself. Usually some like-minded escapee could be found to share one's freedom and to assist with some time-passing exercise until we joined the other pupils going home from school. We sometimes had our little diversions at school too, and I remember one snowy winter's day in particular.

When the teachers left their staffroom after the morning interval there was consternation. The upstairs corridor had pools of water all over it, and the source was obvious – the pupils of fifth and sixth year, whose classrooms were at each end of the corridor with the art-room in between, had been having a snowball fight.

Apart from the fact that according to their classteacher they should be old enough to have more sense than to engage in such childish pastimes, they should at least have known better than to carry loads of ready-made snowballs up the stairs. I was in sixth year at the time and I suppose that fifth year got much the same lecture.

The water was mopped up, the corridor swept, and by the time we broke for lunch everything was nice and dry and back to normal.

When we got back after lunch, however, it was obvious that our teachers had little faith in the efficacy of their lectures of the morning; they just didn't trust us! Posted at the foot of the two sets of stairs were two teachers on sentry duty. Each ascending scholar was carefully scrutinised, and any who came in the main door carrying snowballs, as soon as they saw the sentries, turned on their heels and dumped their loads.

However, we were not to be balked. There was plenty of snow on the roof of the covered way between the main building and the gymnasium, and access looked possible by the window of Class Six room. The only question was, who was to be the ammunition supplier? I suppose I must have been the obvious choice. The previous summer I had taken the all-round athletic championship at the Stornoway Football League Sports, and at the end of the current session I was to take the school gymnastic prize. Anyway I found myself out on the roof passing huge chunks of snow in through the classroom window, so that the battle could go on; and go on it did.

Once again there was dismay when the sentries at the foot of the stairs left their posts and the teachers returned, because the upstairs corridor was as be-puddled with melted snow as it had been in the morning: the source remained a mystery; although some doubt may have been cast on the reliability of the sentries.

Spadework

One spring towards the end of our stay in Newvalley, my brother John and I were engaged to work on a croft in Benside digging the *feannagan* (rigs) with spades for the planting of potatoes, oats and barley. He was on Easter holidays from university and I from school.

It was one of those crofts on the steep slope of Benside where the use of a horse and plough was more or less impossible; and the *sgiobadh* (crew) of five who were doing the spade work included two women. The work was hard, and after an eight-hour day of bending over the spade and turning the sod we needed no lulling to sleep when we tumbled into our beds at night.

The croft belonged to Aonghas Choinnich (Kenneth's Angus) who was then an old man and bedridden. His daughter and son-in-law lived in the house with him and were working the croft.

On the first day of our stint, when we went into the house for our midday meal, Aonghas was in bed in the room in which we were to eat. He was still mentally alert and able to take an interest in all that was happening, and to participate in the mealtime conversation. This was probably why his bed was set in the main room of the cottage, so that he would be able to feel a part of what was going on from day to day.

The other three members of the working crew were all from Benside and known to Aonghas; but my brother John and I were from Newvalley, and also so young that we were complete strangers to the old man. Consequently his first question was a request for identification; John said to him: 'Tha sin le Murchadh 'an Fhionnlaigh a Bragair' – 'We belong to Murdo the son of John the son of Finlay [Finlay's John's Murdo] from Bragar.'

121

Old Aonghas beamed and he said in Gaelic: 'Well! Well! Your grandfather, 'an Fhionnlaigh worked along with me when we were building the concrete sea-front at South Beach. It was a long time ago. And I remember that he was one of the strongest men that I have ever known. The bags of cement were stored on a raised wooden platform to keep them dry, and we carried them as they were required to where the concrete was being mixed. I shall always remember 'an Fhionnlaigh going up to the platform, taking a bag of cement under each arm, and walking away with them. And he wasn't big at all! He wasn't big! But he was strong – strong!'

My grandfather was not a big man. I've been told that he was about 5 feet 8 inches tall; so if he did carry two bags of cement, one under each arm, it was quite a feat.

Aonghas Choinnich was an old man when he told us about it, but I have no reason to suspect from his part in the mealtime conversation that day that there was anything wrong with his mind or his memory.

While engaged in the digging on the croft the work was lightened by banter and snippets of conversation; and my recollection is not of anyone complaining or groaning at such strenuous activity but of quips, anecdotes and laughter.

My brother John always had a fund of little stories and I remember one of his about one picturesque local character, John Macsween. John was a retired ship's fireman, and although now well on in years, he had never succeeded in quenching the consuming thirst originally generated by his work in the stoke hold. But no one could say that he hadn't applied himself, with frequent visits to the town's hostelries where he partook of copious libations of draught beer. On several occasions on his way home from these expeditions he had sustained broken limbs, but although the broken limbs mended the thirst remained.

Now if there was one thing that John detested more than being at home under the watchful eye of a censorious wife (when he could have been in the pub drinking beer) it was being dragooned into working at peats on a hot summer's day, and being kept there safely under surveillance until after closing time.

It was after one of these days at the peats, trudging wearily homewards too late for any hope of irrigating the desert in the back of his throat that his thirst had by then become, that he was met by Murdo (The Nipper) Maciver, who was always ready for a bit of leg-pulling.

'Well, well John,' said The Nipper, exaggerating the surprise, 'You've been at the peats?'

'Yes, Murdo,' disconsolately from John. 'I've been at the peats. Those damned women are never happy unless they're making some poor man miserable.'

'Oh man, John,' from The Nipper with feigned sympathy. 'You stayed very late. They're closed now! And I just saw Calum Fox staggering out the road with three sheets in the wind.'

'Huh!' snorted John, 'It's a damn good thing somebody's drunk, even if I'm not.'

The Uni

Interesting, entertaining and often strenuous as Newvalley life was outside school, nevertheless the requirements of the education machine had to be observed, and a Higher Leaving Certificate must be obtained.

To glorify God may be man's chief end, but for a Nicolson Institute pupil's in my time it was to obtain a

Higher Leaving Certificate, issued on a basis of groupings of passes at higher and lower levels, in certain specified subjects. To this end all efforts were concentrated, and on the number of pupils getting their 'Highers' rested the prestige of the school and the success rating of the teachers.

There were no careers advisers, and that a pupil might finish up with the required passes, but with no clear idea of where he or she might be going from there, did not seem to be a cause for concern. Probably the teaching fraternity, like the brainwashed pupils, took it for granted that apart from the odd exception, the future career would be one of the traditional trinity – Divinity, Medicine and Education.

Sitting the Leaving Certificate examinations was made much more pleasant for me by the generosity of a lady whose kindness and warmth I shall always remember.

One of my classmates was Ian Mackenzie, whose father, D. G. Mackenzie, had a draper's shop in Perceval Square in Stornoway, a shop to which Ian invariably referred, tongue-in-cheek, as 'the emporium'. Ian had a wonderful sense of humour and was ever ready for any ploy likely to end in laughter. So it was not surprising that we spent a lot of time together, and he frequently invited me to his home on Matheson Road. He played the piano, and after a session that could range from Beethoven to the latest popular ditty his mother would entertain me to a sumptuous high tea.

At the time of the Highers she insisted that I should go home with Ian each day instead of making do with a sandwich and a drink of water – my normal lunch time diet at that time – and the delightful immaculately served three-course meals that were presented to me by Mrs Mackenzie during that period I shall never forget; but I remember with greater pleasure the genuine warmth with which she treated me.

I obtained my Leaving Certificate, but missing was a pass in Latin, which, unfortunately, was essential in my grouping for entrance to a university, and it was taken for granted by everyone, including myself, that I would be going to university.

Looking back I can never understand why I did not protest or rebel, but accepted the situation as if it were a *fait accompli*.

So during the summer holidays following my last year at school, in the intervals of working at peats, playing football, training for the annual sports meeting in Willow Glen, boxing bouts with anyone who would put on the gloves with me, I now had to study for a University Preliminary Examination in Higher Latin.

I had never been able to generate any enthusiasm for Latin as a subject, and needless to say I found that having to devote any time at all to it during the long summer days was not so much a tiresome chore as an intolerable penance.

When the Nicolson reopened that year after the summer break, I met the classical master in Cromwell Street. He stopped to pass the time of day and asked me what I was doing; and when I told him that I was studying for my Higher Latin Prelim he shook his head sadly and turned away muttering, 'Mon! Mon! You'll never get a pass in Higher Latin. Never! Never!'

As I walked away from him I thought to myself, 'You don't have to be so damned discouraging! I'll show you whether I can get a pass or not!' I did in fact get a pass the following month, and I sometimes wondered afterwards whether he had said what he did in order to goad me into greater effort.

When I went to Glasgow that September to sit the examination it was my first visit to the mainland of Scotland, and when I stepped off the *Lochness* at Mallaig in the early hours of the morning and walked across to the railway station I saw a train for the first time. This was an early morning journey that was to be repeated many times. When I reached Glasgow I found myself in a strange new environment, an environment with which I became increasingly familiar in subsequent years but to which I was never able to adjust properly. I detested the winter fogs. And in early spring and late autumn (I was always at home during the summer) I would trudge disconsolately along crowded streets dreaming of quiet country roads, open fields and wide moors.

While at university I was most fortunate in that I was lodging with my great-aunt Cairstiona. She was a widow, and living with her were her two daughters and one son. My brother John had lodged there during his four years in Glasgow – three at the university and one at Jordanhill – and consequently she was quite ready to accept me too, on the rather large assumption that I would be just as stable and well-behaved a character as he was. I hope that she was not too disillusioned by the time I left Glasgow.

In addition to being a superlative cook Cairstiona was one of the most generous and open-hearted persons that I have ever known. I was always treated as one of the family and could not have received better attention had I been her own son.

As soon as the first term started I joined the University Harriers and the Ossianic Society; I enjoyed long-distance running, and had also been an enthusiastic participant in the activities of the Nicolson Institute Debating Society. I had many very pleasant outings with the Harriers despite the fact that I often had to walk from my lodgings in Shamrock Street all the way to Westerlands, and back again after the cross-country run, because I didn't have the bus fare.

One occasion that I remember particularly is an outing with Maryhill Harriers, at Maryhill, on a mild, seeping-wet Saturday afternoon, when Dunky Wright and Donny Robertson, both veteran marathon champions, were out with the Maryhill pack. I am happy to remember that in such distinguished company I 'also ran'.

I did not participate very much in Ossianic Society activities, although one winter I did take a leading part in a debate, at very short notice, because the student who had been scheduled to speak to the motion had been killed in a climbing accident. Two things have combined to fix this in my memory: the first being that on that particular Friday night I had such a very heavy feverish cold that I had to leave immediately after finishing my speech without waiting for the debate, and secondly that on the Saturday morning I was approached by Angus Macleod, a Lewis student who later became Director of Education for the Western Isles, with a request for a copy of my speech, because, he said, it was the best that he had ever heard up to then. After such a handsome compliment it was with regret that I had to tell him that I couldn't comply as I had been speaking from notes and didn't have a speech written out.

Some time later I joined the University Socialist Society and attended a number of parliamentary debates in the Union: always, however, as an observer as I was not able to overcome a basic Hebridean reserve.

Towards the end of the first session Johnny Bauer, one of my fellow students who lived in Goathill, told me that my family had moved to 20 Goathill Cottages. As I received at least one weekly letter from home, and as there had been no mention of such a move, I was not quite sure whether I should believe him. My reaction was that Johnny's family, who had sent him the information, were confusing me with someone else.

However when I returned to Lewis (it was at the end of June) I discovered that the family had indeed left Newvalley and moved to Goathill; they had moved in May but had not told me so that I would get a pleasant surprise when I got home.

And what a surprise it was, in spite of my being forewarned. When I reached the new house with the 'reception committee' that had met me when the *Lochness* berthed I couldn't believe my eyes: before even going inside I stood at the front and looked at the upstairs windows, walked round the end (it was the end house in a block of four), stood at the back and looked at the upstairs windows. Then I turned to my father and said, 'Is this all ours?' 'Yes,' he said, laughing at my surprise, 'This is all ours.'

When I went inside I discovered that downstairs consisted of a living room, kitchen, pantry, small store and lavatory. On the stair landing there was a bathroom, and upstairs three bedrooms; I found it difficult to take it all in. After the clay-floored two-roomed thatched hovel that we had occupied for the previous nine years it looked palatial.

It had not been necessary to engage a removal firm for the flitting from Newvalley to Goathill: the complete furnishings of the little cottage were transported quite adequately by horse and cart.

On its arrival in residential suburbia such was the nomadic appearance of the procession – horse, cart, furniture, carter, assorted humans (children and grown-up male and female) – as to persuade one of the Goathill urchins to dash home to inform a startled mother that tinkers had come to live in Number 20!

Although now living in Goathill and quite a distance from Newvalley I continued with my summer holiday work at peats.

The official unemployment figure was still between two and three million, and, as always, the Outer Hebrides was a statistical 'black spot'. So if I were to earn any money I had to turn to the work that was available – and although the Cnoc Mor, Beinne Drobh and the Creagan Loisg were now much further away I went regularly to these working sites, did a full day's work with the barrow, and then walked back to Goathill. On one or two evenings a week I turned out after the day's work for a league or cup-tie game of football.

My day's pay was still five shillings (25p), with breakfast, dinner and tea – but there was an ancillary benefit in that I was superbly fit.

The facilities available at 20 Goathill Cottages as compared with the little thatched hovel at 23 Newvalley made for a much more pleasant home life after the day's work was done, and on the days when no work was available there was the Cockle Ebb; or better still the Broad Bay beach, beyond the Steinish Golf Links, where I spent many pleasant hours swimming and sunbathing.

The only thought that marred the long, strenuous but happy summer days was that of going back to Glasgow to resit degree examinations. This happened with disconcerting regularity while I was at university, and as resits were invariably in September, which is often the most pleasant time of the year in the Outer Hebrides, my resentment at having to leave the island was given additional impetus.

Glasgow was suffering more than its fair share of the deep depression affecting the country's economy at the time, and the obvious poverty, malnutrition and deterioration in social standards inevitably resulting from mass unemployment was most disheartening. Every time that we West Highland and Islands students made the rail journey to and from Glasgow the abandoned, skeletal structure of the 534 (later to be the ocean liner *Queen Mary*), visible in John Brown's shipyard from the windows of the train, was a recurring reminder of the precarious state of the country, and of the insecurity that might be waiting for us in the future. We knew that many of those who had already obtained good degrees and qualifications were either unemployed or being paid a pittance for doing some menial task. On the rare occasions when we paused from our youthful involvement with the present it was with some anxiety that we looked ahead.

Another dismal sight visible from the windows of the Glasgow–Mallaig train was the rusting merchant ships lying deserted in the Gare Loch while far too large a percentage of Britain's merchant seamen couldn't get a berth, and many of the more unfortunate ones had to queue up at soup-kitchens in seaports all round Britain.

Not many years later these same ships and these same seamen were running essential war supplies along convoy routes where they suffered a higher percentage of casualties than did any of the three fighting services – Royal navy, army or air force. When on convoy escort duty during the Second World War I often watched plucky little salt-encrusted steamers butting through rough seas, and knowing how vulnerable they were to attack by U-boat or E-boat, I saw again the rusty empty hulks from the train window, remembering the fine men

1. Author, September 1939 (the month this little story ends)

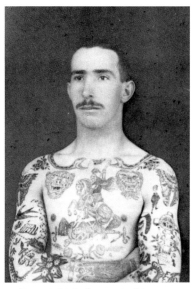

2. 'Duppie' Mackenzie in his tattoos – India, pre-First World War

3. Author and crofter's daughter, Miss Macgregor, planting potatoes, Newvalley croft, circa spring 1932

4. Author's father (standing at back right with moustache) with fellow Naval Reservists, 1914–1918

5. Smith family 1928, Newvalley (author at back on right)

6. Author and future wife in fancy dress, hospital carnival, 1938

7. Three school (Nicolson) football players; back left 'Safety' Smith, Laxdale (author); back right, 'T. C.' Macgregor. Tolstachaolais; seated front, 'Sammy' Morrison, Bragar

8. Peggy Flett, to whom the author was introduced by the Ministry of Labour in 1937 and whom he married in 1942

9. Calum relaxing outdoors

10. Calum and his eldest daughter, Elizabeth

11. Calum circa his journalism days with the ferry and Stornoway beyond

12. Portrait photograph of Calum

13. Calum in 'The Netmender' by his artist brother, Donald, circa 1956

who couldn't get a ship in which to sail, and thought to myself 'It must never be allowed to happen again.'

One of the victims of the economic depression was my landlady's son Peter. He was a ship's carpenter, and although the tools of his trade were honed and oiled ready for use, in a fine toolbox that he had made himself, he hadn't worked for some years. Although he was six years older than I we were great friends, and so I invited him to spend a summer holiday with me in Lewis. It took some persuasion to get him to agree, but he finally did; and when I went back home from university that summer Peter came with me. Fortunately it turned out to be a summer of fine weather with lots of sunshine, and we had a wonderful time. He stayed for several weeks, during which time we lived almost entirely out-of-doors, only returning home for meals, and at night to sleep. When he returned to Glasgow all his friends were complimenting him on how fit and well he looked, and he himself maintained that it was one of his best holidays ever.

While he was in Lewis I went with him one evening to the village of Aignish (actually he was interested in a young lady in that village and wanted moral support) and when we went into the house that he was visiting, the crofter occupier's first question to me was, 'A bheil Gaidhlig agad?'

'Tha,' I replied, 'Lan mo chinn.'

'Co as a tha thu?'

'Tha a Steornabhagh. Ach 's ann a Siabost a rugadh mi. Tha m'athair a Bragar.'

'Bhoil a bhalaich, 'sann dhuit bu choir a bhi cruaidh agus, laidir! Cha robh mise ach aon turus ann am Bragair a riamh, agus bu cho math leum dusan bliadhna dheanamh as na "convicts" ann an Ceannphaduig na mo bhi-beo thoirt aon bliadhna a croit ann am Bragair.'

'Have you got Gaelic?'

'Yes, my head full.'

'Where are you from?'

'From Stornoway. But I was born in Shawbost. My father is from Bragar.'

'Well boy, you should be hardy and strong! I was only once ever in Bragar, and I would rather do a dozen years in the convicts in Peterhead than take my living for one year out of a croft in Bragar.'

Peter was highly diverted by this comment.

I thought that he was exaggerating, but when you compare the lush level fields of Aignish with the rocky outcrops of Bragar you can see his point of view.

When I told him I was from Stornoway I mentioned Shawbost as my birthplace by way of explaining how I came to have 'my head full' of Gaelic (*lan mo chinn* – a common Lewis expression) because very few, if any, of my generation, born in Stornoway of Stornoway parents, were fortunate enough to be fluent Gaelic speakers.

In fact I have a shrewd suspicion that Gaelic speaking was discouraged as being *infra dig* for the 'patricians' of old SY (Stornoway), although almost all of them, like myself, could trace their ancestors all the way back to a leaky-thatched bothy in the lee of a peat-stack.

I remember a friend of mine once giving me an amusing example of how he thought the people of Stornoway spoke Gaelic. 'Bha mi dol spin as a char gun a west side agus fhuair mi puncture. 'S cha robh jack, na tyre-lever, na outfit, na pump, na bugger-all agum!' A translation is unnecessary.

And this is no exaggeration. I myself once overheard a fascinating snippet of conversation. The two speakers were obviously going fishing. One carried on his shoulder a small boat's outboard motor, and the other, in his hand, a basket of ready-baited fishing lines. As I came within earshot the man with the motor was saying: 'Ma tha i cho lan ri sin overflowigidh i.'

To which observation his companion replied: 'Ciod e mar a dh-overflowigeas i, agus i screwed down?'

'If it is as full as that it will over-flow.' 'How will it overflow when it is screwed down?'

13

Grandfather's Donald

A REGULAR VISITOR TO our home in Goathill was my great-uncle Donald Campbell (Domhnull 'An Chaimbeul) from Bragar. Only two years older than my father, and growing up together, in and out of one another's houses, my father always called him 'Domhnull mu sheannar' – 'my grandfather's Donald'; he still referred to him as 'my grandfather's Donald' when they were both old men.

Donald had had a chequered career, and it is no exaggeration to say that among his family, relations and friends he had become a legend in his own lifetime. It is a matter of record that he served with the Seaforth Highlanders in Egypt, with the Cameron Highlanders in the First World War, and that the end of the Second World War found him doing stag duty as a private in the Gordon Highlanders. I have been told that he was a private in the Cameron Militia, a rating in the Royal Naval Reserve and a deserter from the Black Watch all at one and the same time.

One yarn, possibly apocryphal, is that on reporting to one army depot as a recruit he was accosted by an officer from Lewis, who knew him and knew his reputation, with the question, 'Well Donald! And what's your name this time?'

Donald came to attention, saluted smartly, and replied with a deadpan face, 'David Macleod, sir!'

He had now become religious, and was travelling to communion services all over Lewis with the same dedication as that with which he had traipsed all over the North American continent in his younger days. That Donald should take to religion was certainly a turn-up for the book, and I was told that when my cousin Norman Macaulay from Shawbost (described in his obituary as 'a benevolent atheist') heard about it he remarked, 'He's getting old, and his blood is getting thin!'

There is also a story that he was at a communion service in Point where the Reverend Murdo Macrae, who was the Free Church minister at Kinloch, was preaching, and that when he was leaving the church the Reverend Macrae clapped him on the back with the remark, 'Well Donald! You've done a right-about-face yourself I see' – they had been in the Seaforth Highlanders together.

So many tales are told about Donald that one suspects that some of them were made up by family and friends in much the same way as the Irish make up stories about themselves.

It was when going to or coming from the communion in the Point district or when at the Stornoway communions that he stayed with us in Goathill. And knowing his notoriety I was anxious to learn of some of his experiences at first hand. However, I found that he was decidedly reticent and quite unprepared to expatiate on his past adventures. It was only on one occasion that I succeeded in getting any information out of him, and then only because I tackled him directly. Even then the replies were laconic in the extreme.

'Donald!' I said. 'That time you disappeared in 1926 and we didn't hear of you again until you stepped off the mail steamer in Stornoway in 1932 – where did you go?'

'All over the place,' said Donald.

'We heard that you had been seen in the army canteen in Aldershot in '26, but nothing after that.'

'Uh-huh! I would have been there.'

'Did you go to America?'

'Uh-huh!'

'Did you go to Canada?'

'Yes mate! I went to Canada.' Then he must have decided to relent and satisfy my curiosity.

'Nothing doing here. No work. Nothing much in England either. Picked up a berth on a tramp steamer bound for Baltimore. Jumped ship. Different jobs. Had to get out. Not an American citizen. Got a berth on a Havana bound cargo boat. Jumped ship again and stayed there a while. From there went to New Orleans. Working my passage. Decided to hitchhike to Montreal.'

Here I interrupted him in sheer amazement. I didn't know offhand what the distance was but I thought it must be in the region of 1,500 miles.

'Hitchhike from New Orleans to Montreal!'

'The Americans. Very good at giving lifts,' said Donald.

'And if you had good stories. Jokes. Make them laugh. Take you hundreds of miles sometimes. Even buy meals for you at transport cafés. Feed you. They were all right.'

Here he paused, and as I was anxious for him to go on

I prompted him with the question 'And did you make it to Montreal?'

'No! Changed my mind. About three hundred miles from Montreal. Decided on California.'

Again I was astonished. 'And did you make it to California?'

'Uh-huh! Then Seattle. Vancouver. Winnipeg. Montreal.'

There was another pause.

'And after that?' I said.

'After that!' he said. 'Came home.'

That was the longest and most elaborate dissertation on his own adventures that I ever got from my globetrotting great-uncle, but I am sure that his life story, if it were available, would make fascinating reading.

Incidentally there was some corroborative evidence of his North American wanderings. I understand that one Lewisman reported that he had seen Donald acting as commissionaire at the entrance of a cinema in Baltimore. And Sandy Mackay, who worked with me in the Ministry of Labour in Stornoway, told me that he had seen him as foreman on a construction job in Montreal.

I do not think that I have ever met anyone who knew him who did not have some amusing tale to tell about him.

My father told me that he was once in the same crew with Donald on a Moray coast herring drifter. He himself was working as a 'hired man' and Donald was cook.

One morning the drifter skipper and my father were going to grease the mast, but couldn't find the round metal tin with the tallow used for the purpose. They were searching high and low when Donald emerged from the galley, and realising that they were looking for something said, 'Dhia mhate! And what are you looking for?'

He had a conversational habit of prefacing almost all his utterances with the mild Gaelic expletive 'Dhia mhate' – 'God mate!'

'We're looking for the grease for the mast,' said the skipper.

'Dhia mhate!' said Donald, 'And what does it look like?'

'It was a round metal tin,' the skipper gesticulated with his hands. 'About so big, and so deep – full of grey-white tallow.'

'Dhia mhate!' said Donald, with a fiendish grin. 'You needn't bother looking any more. You've been eating that in dumplings for the past fortnight.'

My father, who had a squeamish stomach at the best of times, made a dive for one rail and started retching; and the skipper, who apparently wasn't much better, dived for the other rail and retched an accompaniment. While Donald did a jig back into his galley, calling as he went 'Dhia mhate! You're too bloody late now mates!'

A couple of days later a member of the crew found the full tin of tallow in a remote corner where it should never have been. But Donald had had his laugh.

14

The hare

_____

A T GOATHILL MY FATHER was finding life much more pleasant than it had been for many years, (as we all were). In the (comparatively) spacious sitting room at Number 20 he could read his book in the evening in peace and comfort without having someone bump into him or stumble over him.

When reading he had an inordinate capacity for concentration. He could become so absorbed in a book that it was almost impossible to distract him.

One afternoon my mother came back from shopping in town and found the back door open. The doors from the back lobby to the kitchen and from the kitchen to the sitting room were open too, as was the door from the sitting room to the front lobby. My father was in his fireside chair reading, but the fire was out.

She closed the back door and put her shopping away. She closed both kitchen doors, walked through the sitting room, went upstairs to put her coat away, came down stairs, closed the sitting room door, crossed the sitting room floor and sat down in the fireside chair opposite him. He was still oblivious, after all that, of the world about him, and it was some moments after she sat down before he came back to earth and realised he was no longer alone. He put down the book, grabbed the poker, and began poking the ashes of the dead fire. Then he looked at her over his glasses and said, 'I'm afraid the fire is out!'

On another occasion I came in myself and he was in his chair reading, with my mother in the opposite chair knitting.

I spoke to my mother; and then to him, but got no reply. I spoke to him again – and again, but still got no answer. So I went into the kitchen, got a medium-sized paper bag and blew it up, and took it into the sitting room.

My mother looked at me in horror and said, 'You mustn't do that!'

I said, 'Why not? He's away in a world of his own and we must bring him back!'

Father was still reading away quite unconscious of all that was going on around him. So I burst the paper bag behind his head.

The consequences were spectacular – the book flying across the room, the spectacles jumping off his nose, and not least the explosive 'Isean a reabhaich!' ('You child of the Devil') when he realised as he bounced to his feet that I was responsible. But within seconds he was sitting back laughing as I said, 'But I spoke to you three times and you didn't answer!'

When not reading he liked nothing better than to start some discussion which he would keep under control with incisive comments or calls to order. And in which he would participate most effectively when he chose. He not only had the capacity for lucid argument but also for the expressive word or phrase. When using his mother tongue, Gaelic, he had a special facility.

One evening, when there was no-one in but the two of us we were sitting on either side of the fire, each engrossed in his own book, when there was a knock at the door. It was John Campbell (Iain a' Rollair) collecting the 'sustentation' fund for the Free Church. He came in and sat down; he and my father were from neighbouring villages and as they talked I picked up my book, at the same time taking in bits and pieces of the conversation.

Then, as has been the way of churchmen in all ages, John made some remark about the waywardness of the younger generation, and my father, ever ready to defend the friendless, said, 'Now John, you know very well that if boys today did some of the things that we got up to when we were young, you in Arnol and I in Bragar, they would be up on Lewis Street answering in court for their misdeeds.'

'Oh well, Murdo,' admitted John with a smile, 'I don't know but that you're quite right.' And then the reminiscing began, most of which I missed because my attention was divided between my book and their talk. However, there was one part of the conversation that I remembered for the rest of my life. It was when my father said, 'Tha cuimhne agam s'a a bhi tighinn dhachaidh bho na mointeach aon fheasgair sabaid, agus chuir sinn suas gearr; 's cha b'urrainn na b'fhearr ach toiseachadh dha ruith; ruith sinn e, chro sin e, rug sin air, mharbh sinn e, fheann sinn e, bhrieos sinn e, rinn sinn brot air, 's dhith sinn e, 's chuir sin a chreacan aig air a chat ma's d'thainig mo sheanair as a choinneamh.' ('I remember coming home from the moor one Sunday evening and we put up a hare, and there was nothing better than to begin chasing it; we chased it, we penned it, we caught it, we killed it, we skinned it, we cooked it and made broth with it, and we ate it, and we put its skin on the cat before my grandfather came from the meeting.') It was a saga in one sentence.

He didn't say why they fitted the skin of the hare on the cat, but I feel sure that there was some poor superstitious soul in Bragar that night who thought that either a witch or the devil himself was having a frolic.

But if things were vastly improved for the rest of us they must have constituted a revolution for my mother. She must have found it a different world – the additional living space, bathroom facilities, hot and cold water on tap, a gas cooker instead of an open peat-fire.

Looking back and making comparisons I shall never be able to understand how, as the family kept increasing and the living space remained static, with no sanitation, no running water and open-fire cooking, she coped with the circumstances in which she previously had to work, and managed to keep us all in good heart.

15

Valtos

BACK HOME FROM university in 1936 as an unrepentant 'dropout', with no degree or qualification, my chances of obtaining any work were almost non-existent.

University graduates with good degrees and teaching certificates were either digits in the unemployment statistics or were earning a pittance doing all kinds of odd jobs as drudges, ordinary seamen on tramp steamers, labourers, clerks – any work that they could get.

There were two and a half million unemployed at the time and millions of those working were on starvation wages. Sir John Boyd Orr, the world-renowned expert on the subject, maintained that approximately twenty million people in Great Britain were suffering to some degree from malnutrition.

In those good old days there were no social security payments for school leavers or unemployed students or graduates, and consequently they just became an additional burden on family incomes that were already, in many cases, hopelessly inadequate.

With the prevailing climatic conditions a Hebridean winter can be pretty grim, even for those who are well set up to cope with it; and for me that winter at home was one of utter frustration, and a nagging consciousness of inadequacy. My time indoors was spent reading; but I also spent many hours out of doors, whatever the weather, walking miles every day.

It was at the end of this winter that I was invited to Uig for the second time by John Buchanan. He was returning home to Valtos after completing his course for a teaching certificate – he had already taken an MA degree at Glasgow University.

John and I had started at the Nicolson at the same time sharing the front seat at a row of desks in class IA, and after being classmates for six years we had gone to university together.

I had already spent a short summer break at Valtos – a typical Atlantic coast Hebridean village with sandy beaches, imposing cliffs and productive crofts – with him, and after a long weary winter of idleness I was more than pleased to accept his kind invitation to go there again.

On my first visit we were on holiday from Glasgow University and I had managed to snatch a fortnight from the grind of peat-ferrying day-work. The pay was still five shillings a day, and every shilling I could earn was needed to supplement the County bursary which amounted to £32. As approximately £28 of this was spent on lodgings the £4 left over did not go far towards meeting other commitments. So the day-work that I had started as a schoolboy of fifteen still went on during my so-called holidays from university.

As soon as I got to Valtos Angus Macaulay (Aonghas Iain Mhurchaidh Bhuidhe) called to see me. Angus' grandfather, Murdo Macaulay, and my great-grandfather, Malcolm Macaulay, were brothers, and family ties in Lewis demanded that the relationship, although distant, should be recognised and acknowledged. John Buchanan and I were invited to high tea.

During the meal the conversation, as always with Angus, was loud and bright, and after he had treated us to an entertaining dissertation on the history of the Macaulays, where the exploits of our mutual ancestor Donald Cam featured prominently, he took time off to ask me what subjects I was studying at Glasgow. When I mentioned Latin (I never did study it although it was included in my curriculum) he said that he had done Latin at elementary school, and to prove it he recited excerpts from Caesar's *Gallic War* from memory, translating as he went along.

Not only was I surprised that Latin should have been taught in a remote elementary school in the wilds of Uig at the end of the nineteenth century, but I was so lost in admiration for his power of recall that I exclaimed, quite forgetting the respect due to his age, and much to his wife's amusement, 'Well! give the devil his due, he's good.'

'He's got his proper title at last – devil!' said his wife, laughing.

Then Angus went on with further demonstrations of his astonishing memory, as apparently he could recollect with almost script-like precision anything that had riveted his attention.

There is one account in particular that I remember because of a phrase that was used. He told us that he went to his first communion at the age of fifteen, to Carloway. Then he went on to give us the text from which the minister had preached his Sunday morning sermon, and the way in which the text had been expounded – introduction, headings, conclusion. Of all of this I remember nothing, except for one phrase that the minister had used during the sermon, and which must have impressed me as much as the whole sermon did Angus. It was 'Tha gras Dhe mar tha an cuan mor. Tha e air son neart bheag a chudaig mar tha e air son neart mhor na muic mhara.' – 'The grace of God is like the great ocean. It is for the tiny strength of the minnow as it is for the great strength of the whale.'

That evening was one of the highlights of my visit to Valtos. Angus was a boisterous extrovert character whose voice even in ordinary conversation reverberated in the rafters and echoed back off the walls, and he had most assuredly inherited the Celtic capacity for making entertaining conversation.

Now on a second occasion I was back in Uig with John, and received the same generous welcome and hospitality from his mother, sister and two brothers as I had done the first time.

Once more I was involved with my cousin Angus Macaulay, and other five Valtos men were involved as well, in an incident that nearly cost us our lives.

Preparations had been made for a fishing expedition. Angus' boat had been got ready for sea. The small lines were baited, and I was invited to join the party. We were up with the dawn, and ignoring the warning menace of a rose-pink sky we set off out of the Caolas (the narrows between Valtos and the island of Pabbay) for the Atlantic.

Off Gallan Head we began paying out the baited lines, but by this time the wind had freshened considerably from the south-west. So as soon as the last set of lines went over the side we went back to haul the first lot. In they came, with a fish on every hook, large haddocks, sole and plaice; but as the lines were hauled and the hooks cleared it was quite amazing how rapidly and how violently the weather was deteriorating. It was now blowing a gale, and with the strong ebb-tide current that is a feature off Gallan Head, it was driving us out into the Atlantic. There were one or two glances skywards from the working crew, a few quiet words, out came a knife and the line was cut. A marker buoy was attached to the abandoned lines. We were going to run for it.

The wind had risen to such a menacing pitch that they decided rather than risk the sail to row into the lee of the land. Out went the oars and I was asked to take the tiller. Although I couldn't hope to hold my own with an oar in that company I could be trusted to hold a steady course. I was given instructions to take a bearing on Mangersta Head off the Gallan, and to report on the headway being made by the rowers. I let them pull away for about five minutes. Then I reported that they were holding the boat against the wind and tide, but making no progress.

'Och,' said Angus, 'won't you listen to the *amadan* [clown]! Go and have a look, Murdo.' So Murdo Smith [Murchadh a' Ghobha] came into the stern, checked the bearing and said, 'The lad is right enough. We're just where we started.'

It was agreed then that the sail must be tried. There was no alternative. So with all points reefed the little brown lug sail was hoisted and we headed for the *seanna bheinn*. But now Murchadh a' Ghobha took the tiller.

The wind had risen to a howling gale, driving clouds of spin drift off the wave crests, and even with minimum sail we were racing with the port gunwale awash. Soon we were kept busy bailing, and we were all drenched to the skin with spray.

Before coming about on the return tack allowance had to be made for the strength of the current and the consequent seaward drift. However, when we did come about and had sailed for some time it was found that we had miscalculated, and that if we carried on we would be driven out beyond Gallan Head, instead of making the lee of the cliffs at Aird, as we had hoped. So we just had to try again, and it was as the sail was being hoisted for the next tack that Angus looked up, his bristling eyebrows beaded with spray, and bellowed in his normal voice that defied any wind: 'Oh well, I hope the halyard doesn't break. I was going to replace it last summer but I didn't get round to it.'

Murchadh a' Ghobha smiled quietly, shook his head slowly, and said, 'Just listen to him! This is a great time to be telling us that.' The response from the rest of us was grins all round, although we all knew that if the halyard did go we wouldn't have a hope. In fact it was becoming apparent even to a person as inexperienced as I that even if the halyard didn't give way we still had quite a lot to do if we were to make it back to Valtos.

But Murchadh a' Ghobha at the tiller was getting the maximum out of the little craft, and when we next came about we made the lee of the land below Aird. Once we got into the sheltered water under these huge cliffs it was like being in a different world.

There was a brief consultation. Would we beach the boat and walk from Aird to Valtos, or would we make our way under oars to Cliff and then risk sailing across to clear the point at Valtos and into the Caolas. The run across the bay from Cliff to Valtos was short, but the wind was being funnelled through the gap with an additional violence that tore the wave crests into white curtains of spin drift.

The Valtos men decided against the walk from Aird, however. I am quite sure that the decision was against the long walk rather than for the short dangerous sail.

(And I should say here that I had no part in any of these consultations or decisions, apart from a courteous query as to whether I agreed, as I was very much the novice as well as being, I think, the youngest in the boat.)

So once more the oars were out, and I was asked again to take the tiller. But once we got into position to hoist the sail I reverted to my amateur status of being only a passenger.

Even with a rag of sail we screamed across that bay, and although by no means out of danger it was a most exhilarating run. Once we cleared the point at Valtos and got into the lee of the land we were home and dry. Down came the sail, out went the oars, and for the third time that day the tiller was given to Calum.

Murchadh a' Ghobha was sitting beside me in the stern and he leaned sideways and said quietly, 'Calum, make some comment about how cold it would be in the sea just now.' I knew by his expression that some game was afoot, so I said in loud clear tones, 'Well, I wouldn't care to find myself in the waters of the Caolas at this time of year. It must be bitterly cold.'

'Huh!' snorted Angus, making it quite obvious why I had been briefed by Murdo, 'When I was your age I didn't think anything of it. I remember two of us being up there' – pointing to the cliff top – 'in the month of February, cold, with showers of hail, and we saw a sheep caught on a ledge at the foot of the cliff. We got a length of rope and a few potatoes, and I told the boy who was with me to lower the potatoes to me in my cap when I was ready. Then I stripped, dived into the sea and swam to the ledge. I coaxed the sheep towards me with the potatoes, secured it, and it was hauled up the cliff. The rope was lowered again, I tied it round my waist, and between climbing and being hauled made my way up after the sheep. The whole thing didn't bother me one bit.'

This was what Murdo had been angling for, and now he came in with 'Listen to that now Calum. What an *amadan*! Can you imagine anyone who is supposed to possess a scrap of sense putting his own life in danger for the sake of a sheep? I'm sure you've never heard such foolishness in your life.'

Soon everyone in the boat was arguing and laughing. After the hours of strain we were not so much relaxed as light-headed.

We beached the boat on the sand at Valtos quay. The oars were shipped. I stowed the rudder and tiller, and stepping from the stern, thwart by thwart, I jumped from the stem clear of the water on to the sand, where a number of people were waiting. When the sudden storm had blown up anxious villagers had taken to the cliff-tops looking out for us; and we were such a tiny speck in that maelstrom of wind and motion that they couldn't see us until we got close inshore. It was quite a relief when we did appear.

Among those waiting on the beach was Angus' brother, 'Clergy' Macaulay; he was a retired policeman, and a big heavily-built man. When I jumped ashore he looked me in the eye and asked:

'Na chuir a muir ort?' – 'Were you seasick?'

'Cha do chuir.' – 'I wasn't seasick.'

'Na gho thu feagal?' – 'Were you afraid?'

'Cha do gho.' – 'I wasn't afraid.'

He then turned to his brother Angus and repeated the questions.

'Was he seasick?'

'No, he wasn't seasick.'

'Was he afraid?'

'If he was, he didn't show it.'

'Clergy' then turned to me and saying, 'Ni thu chuis a bhalaich.' – 'You'll do lad,' he gave me a thump between the shoulder blades that nearly knocked me face down in the sand.

When I got back to John Buchanan's house – his oldest brother, Malcolm, was in the boat – the first requirement was a change of clothing; and when I stripped, my whole body was covered with a white dusting of salt from the dried-out drenchings of spray.

We had left Valtos about 7.50 in the morning and we beached at 3.30 in the afternoon – eight hours in a small open boat, and most of that time in conditions of extreme exposure. It was not surprising that some went straight to bed after their ordeal.

Part of Malcolm Buchanan's share of the catch provided an excellent meal of haddock and *ceann gropaig* with mealy potatoes; after which, being young and fit, I was out and about that evening as if nothing had happened.

There were some in the village who voiced the opinion that what we had suffered was largely our own fault, by going to sea when the signs were so ominous – after all it was a Uig woman, who, when asked what were the three things she feared most, made the first item 'Ros na maidne' – 'A red dawn.' But it was agreed that we were fortunate to escape with our lives: no Valtos boat had been that far out in the Atlantic in such conditions in living memory, and it was an incident that was talked about for a long time.

In fact about a quarter of a century later I was crossing the Minch in one of MacBrayne's ferries and got talking to a man from Valtos, and in the course of our conversation I mentioned that I knew the village and some of the villagers. When I named some of the men who had been with me in the boat he looked surprised and said, 'Were you in that boat, in that storm?' Although he lived and worked on the mainland and only went to Uig for holidays obviously he had heard all about it.

A few days after the expedition Angus asked me whether I had understood the danger, suggesting that I was too inexperienced to have realised our peril. So I told him that I had been well aware of the hazards of our situation, and somewhat indignantly suggested in return that I would have to be all kinds of a fool not to. He then said, 'Well, what were you going to do if the boat had gone down?'

'I'll tell you,' I said. 'I had been keeping a lookout to sea, because I had noticed that trawlers often operated in that area; but there wasn't a sign of a ship or a wisp of smoke, so there was no help in that direction. And with the wind and current as they were that's the direction in which I'd be going if I ended up in the sea. So I could see no hope of surviving in the waters of the Atlantic at that time of year with no help available, and I had made up my mind not to prolong the agony. I was saying to myself, "If she is swamped or capsizes I must try to reach the bottom as fast as I can, to get it over with!"'

'Oh nach eisd thu,' shouted Angus, 'ma's fhalbh a Satan leat!' – 'Oh be quiet, in case Satan takes you away!'

There were two things that made a great impression on me that day. The first was at the very beginning of the storm, when, without a word being said by any of the other six men in the boat, Murchadh a' Ghobha asked me to take the tiller, and I realised that this was being done so that I would feel that I was accepted as one of the crew. At such a time of stress it was a supreme gesture of Hebridean courtesy. The second was the calm steadiness of every man, even at the worst moments. They all knew the score, but, as Angus had said on the beach, they 'didn't show it'.

16

Farm hand

THAT SPRING I GOT a job – for which I had no
qualification other than a crofting background, and a
willingness to tackle anything. I became a farm labourer
on the Macaulay Farm.

The Macaulay Farm was an experiment in reclaiming
peat land for farming purposes, and was funded by T. B.
Macaulay of the Sun Life Assurance Company of Canada
– a Canadian whose forebears originally came from the
Uig district of Lewis. The farm was sited on the deepest
peatland (acres of it were many feet deep) that could be
found in the vicinity of Stornoway, on the principle that if
such land could be converted to productive farming then
reclamation should be possible anywhere in the island.

It was here that I started my post-university working
career. My hours were to be 6 a.m. to 6 p.m. with a half-
hour break at 8 a.m. for breakfast and an hour break for
dinner at 12 noon. Sunday was to be a half-day – after
the byres were mucked out, that is, and the cows fed and
milked, the store cattle fed and watered. Almost every

day some odd job cropped up that had to be attended to in the evening, so that it was rarely that the working day finished at 6 p.m.

My weekly wage was 30 shillings, and as I was 'living in' 20 shillings of that was paid for my lodgings, which were in the grieve's house. The grieve was Donald (Keose) Macaulay, and I could not have been better treated or better fed than I was by his wife Dolina. How she did it on the miserable 20 shillings a week (two-thirds of my total wages) that I paid I still cannot understand.

The hours were long, the work was hard, the food was good, and in a very short time I was superbly fit, although physically fined down to the leanness of the proverbial rake.

One of the coldest jobs that I have ever done was ploughing with a tractor that spring. Sitting on the tractor (no cabins in those days) in a light pair of trousers, an open-necked shirt and a sports jacket, with no protective layer of insulating fat on my bony frame, buffeted by showers of sleet and hail, it's a wonder I didn't perish. But I don't think hypothermia had been invented then – although some people must have died of it!

Using a tractor on this farm could be a hazard because of the deep soft peat, and on one occasion I was the unfortunate victim. I was taking a small load across a field when I felt the tractor sinking beneath me. It was one of the old heavy variety with caterpillar tracks, and having no experience of such a situation I immediately went into reverse, only to sink deeper. I tried going forward once more but instead went further down into what was rapidly becoming a black morass. Concluding that if I kept up these efforts I would probably disappear without trace I cut out the engine, dismounted and trudged back to the steading.

The farmer, Joe Black, went out with me to inspect the position, and then the salvage team went into action. Past experience had taught its lessons, and the farmer and the grieve knew exactly what to do. But this situation was somewhat worse than usual, because I, by my inexperience had dug the machine deep into the peat.

Three railway sleepers and a Weston pulley (endless chain in farm language) were carried to the scene. Two of the railway sleepers were driven vertically into the peat, in a strategic position, leaving enough of them above ground for the third sleeper to be lashed across them. The Weston pulley was secured to the crosspiece and on to the tractor. Then the slow, laborious hauling began, inch by painful inch – until we started pulling the sleepers out of the peat: they were then driven down in a new position, and the agonising process started all over again. I don't know just how long it took us to get that machine on to firm ground but I'm sure that it took hours.

We had just got back to the farm and were preparing for the evening milking when there was a cry from the farmer's wife: 'The engine is on fire!'

It was a petrol engine housed in a concrete cubicle with a cement floor, just big enough to hold the engine and little else.

I happened to be nearest when the call came, and as I dashed out of the byre I saw the flames spreading over the engine-room floor (on which there was always a layer of water) as the floating petrol burned.

Making a dive for a heap of hessian sacks that were kept handy for different purposes I clutched a double armful to my chest and dumped the lot in the nearest pool of water; there are always pools of water in Lewis at that time of year. This one happened to be at the lower end of the dung-heap from which a highly concentrated and odoriferous essence percolated into the pool. I jumped on top of the sacks in my Wellington boots to stamp them wet, snatched them up once more in a double armful and dashed for the engine-room, where I started throwing them on top of the engine and beating out the flames.

Then someone clutched the back of my jacket and pulled, and I heard Mrs Black's voice shouting at me: 'Calum, Calum, come out of there before you get killed. It'll blow up!'

It was she who had a hold of me – and she was taking a chance herself; but by that time the fire was nearly out so I kept beating at it with the wet sacks until there were no more flames.

Mrs Black thought I was very brave dashing in as I did to put out the flames, but I wasn't – I was just stupid. It hadn't even occurred to me that the petrol tank might explode, and by the time she had drawn my attention to it the fire was nearly out anyway.

But I had got myself in a mess! Hair and eyebrows singed, blackened with soot from the smoke, and saturated with smelly ooze from the dung-heap – it was very generous of the grieve's wife to let me find my way to the bathroom. She should have insisted that the water-hose be turned on me before letting me near the house.

And that evening, after the hours of hauling on the endless chain, I felt I could count every muscle in my body by counting the aches that I had all over me.

When I first started work at the Macaulay Farm, Joe Black, the farm manager, was laid up recovering from a bout of pneumonia, and the day after I started the grieve asked me to water the Ayrshire bull. This bull was housed in a concrete pen with a sectioned door, the top and bottom halves of which could be opened independently.

When I went to check that the wooden drinking tub was empty and clean, before fetching the water, I found the top half of the door open. So I went and collected a milk-churn full of water, opened the lower half of the door and strode in confidently, elbowing the head of the bull (he was looking at me rather suspiciously) out of my way. I emptied the churn into the tub and he drank thirstily while I watched; when he started licking the bottom of the tub I went for another churnful of water. He polished that off too.

I remarked to the grieve that the bull appeared to be very thirsty and he laughed and said that possibly someone had forgotten to give him water the previous day.

I attended to him daily after that. Sometimes he gave me what I thought was a wicked look, but I just slapped him to one side. This went on until Joe Black got back to work, and it was only then that the grieve told me, with a disarming grin, that everyone on the farm, except Joe Black himself, was terrified of the bull. That was why the top half of the sectioned door of the pen was open – they fed him through there while keeping the bottom half firmly shut.

'And you let me go into that pen with him every day!' I was highly indignant. 'I might have been killed. And the tether tying him to that stall – he could have broken it by shaking his head!'

'Oh,' said Donald, 'you didn't know he was dangerous, so I knew that you wouldn't be afraid of him. And he would know that you were not afraid, so I thought you'd be safe enough!'

It could be, if there were any substance to his farmyard psychology, that it was the confident bliss of ignorance that saved me. But now that I knew the score I unashamedly joined the ranks of those who would not go into that bull's pen for a king's ransom.

The work was hard, the hours were long and the pay was small; but the company was good and I enjoyed working on the Macaulay Farm. In fact I was sorry to leave it.

The farm was never viable. The huge depth of sodden peat absorbed everything in the way of treatment that was lavished on it at great expense. To the outsider the treated area was deceptively green compared with the surrounding brown wasteland.

But the late Charlie (Barley) Macleod, who managed it at one time, once remarked to me that if, yard for yard, as high a concentration of sand and fertiliser was put on the tarmac road running alongside the farm, a better crop of grass would grow on the tarmac.

The reclamation experiment was abandoned, but that was some years after my time there.

But every Lewisman knows that peatland can be reclaimed, as has been proved conclusively by industrious 'squatters' on the fringes of almost every village in Lewis. Crops of potatoes, vegetables, oats, barley, and hay were harvested from 'skinned land' taken over by the disinherited who were making homes for themselves after the two world wars. For this process, however, the main deposit of peat must first be removed.

17

The burroo

I LEFT THE MACAULAY FARM in April 1937 to take up a temporary post in the Employment Exchange in Stornoway.

Unemployment was flourishing at the time (nothing very much else was) and for the Stornoway 'Labour' Exchange a pool of first-class clerical labour was available at pitifully low wages. In the two and a half years that I worked as a 'buroo' clerk five university graduates (one of them with an honours degree) worked along with me as 'temporaries'.

When I first joined the Ministry of Labour ranks the establishment was housed at Battery Point in premises that had been occupied originally by the Royal Naval Reserve when there was a training base in Stornoway.

By today's standards working conditions were primitive. Some of the staff actually sat on chairs, at tables, while working. But I, and a number of others sat on tall rickety wooden stools at long scarred white-wood benches under high-set windows.

Here we applied ourselves to the computation of payments due, the preparation of payment sheets, and the various bits and pieces of simple routine office work. This was so organised – payment over the counter being made on the same day (Friday) each week, and postal payment sheets being sent to head office in Edinburgh on the same day each week – that for half the week we were working like berserk beavers and for the other half we were virtually twiddling our thumbs.

In the time that I worked there I must have spent thousands of man hours doing nothing more demanding or constructive (but how frustrating) than thumping a 'STORNOWAY' rubber stamp on the bottom right-hand corner of hundreds of thousands of buff envelopes. The alleged purpose of this exercise was to save the time required to write 'STORNOWAY' longhand when it came to addressing envelopes to postal claimants. In actual fact it was an elaborate device built into the system to create the impression that we were working.

I often thought that if I had been able to fathom the time and motion implications of this set-up I could have written a thesis on it for a PhD.

When we were going like dynamos to meet the payments deadline I enjoyed the work, but the envelope-stamping slack periods each week, when the supervisory emphasis was on looking busy, nearly drove me screaming up the walls. This was an aspect of the situation to which I could not become reconciled – that although the manager, the section supervisor and everyone else knew that some of us had nothing to do nevertheless we must appear to be doing something.

You looked at the clock, looked at a box of buff envelopes and tried to calculate at what speed the hand with the rubber stamp must be moved from the ink-pad to its destination in order to create the impression, until it was time to go home, you were working.

It was maddening, but it was a job. And with about two and a half million persons getting only their weekly dole a job with a weekly wage, however frustrating at times, was something to hold on to.

I and other members of the staff tried to mitigate the boredom of the idle periods by starting discussions and arguments, carried on in discreet undertones. Sometimes the discreet undertones became declamatory in the friendly heat of disagreement, and then there would be an admonitory intervention by the supervisor, terminating the discussion and reinstating the boredom.

Our section supervisor had been an army sergeant at the latter end of the war, and he had a habit of terminating instructions, especially those of a disciplinary nature, with a clipped military-sounding, 'That's an order.' Only he didn't say 'order', he said 'ohder', giving the final letter 'r' an authentic Scottish burr, but substituting the English 'h' for the first 'r' in the word.

I remember Sandy Mackay, one of my colleagues, having been the recipient of the admonition on one occasion, raising a quizzical eyebrow and remarking 'I can't smell anything.'

'Like what?' I asked.

'Well,' said Sandy, with a characteristic shrug and lopsided grin, 'he did say that was an odour.'

There was one everlasting benefit that I derived from becoming involved with the Employment Exchange.

Towards the end of 1937, the year that I started work there, I was approached by the manager one Friday afternoon, and he asked me whether as my home was in the Goathill area of the town, I would call at 70 Nicolson Road and tell Miss Margaret Isobel (Peggy) Flett that there was a vacancy for her on the Exchange staff and that she could report for work the following Monday morning.

He explained that there was a letter of appointment in process of preparation but that possibly it might not reach Miss Flett in time for a Monday morning start.

Of course I agreed, called at Nicolson Road on the way home and asked for Miss Flett. When she came to the door – a vital, rosy-cheeked, brown-eyed, raven-haired eighteen-year-old – I gave her the message; and I shall always remember how her face lit up at the prospect of a job. She had left school that year with a Higher Leaving Certificate, and was a medallist in English, French and German, but in spite of a brilliant school career a university education was beyond her means, as it was for many others at that time.

Almost exactly five years after I knocked on that door, we were married: and have lived happily together ever since.

In 1938 we (that is, the Stornoway Office of the Ministry of Labour) moved into new premises on Francis Street that had been custom built to our requirements. This location was much more convenient from the point of view of access, and provided working conditions in sharp contrast with those at Battery Point.

Sandy Mackay, whom I have already mentioned, once described the Battery Point office as 'a wooden shack where brown wrapping paper is used in lieu of note paper'. He was annoyed at the time, but as Sandy's previous operational environment had been the air-conditioned premises of the Sun Assurance Company of Canada in Montreal, he must have felt the contrast as sharply as if he had moved from a mansion to a slum. And perhaps he could be excused for his derisory comment.

In the new building we had more, and much more salubrious, working room; and at the same time were more in touch with one another. This made it easier to have our quiet talks during the idle periods.

Now we even had an inside lavatory, and a wash-hand basin; but we still had no hot water, although we did have coal-fired central heating. A gas-heated geyser for the provision of hot water was subsequently installed in 1939, beside the wash-hand basin, but only after some controlled agitation.

Although working conditions had improved there was no change in the work routine. We were still caught in the stop–go rut. Fortunately I had working with me as fine and friendly a group of men as could be gathered under one roof, and it was only the companionship and give-and-take between us all that made it possible for me to put up with the recurring periods of stamp-thumping that I looked upon as nothing more or less than idleness. The times when I was bashing my brains out to beat the clock I could stand without complaint.

The companionship of active service in war has always been extolled in retrospect by many of the fortunate survivors. I may have been unlucky, but during nearly five years of war service I never did experience camaraderie to compare with that experienced in the Stornoway Labour Exchange in 1937, '38 and '39.

And during the war, apart from bursts of frenetic activity, most of my time was spent being utterly bored. The Labour Exchange had been very much better in that the periods of boredom were shorter and the periods of action more frequent.

So, with Sandy Mackay, John Macdonald, Cohn F. Macdonald, Murdo Kerr, Ian Maclean, John Maclennan, Dolly Maclean, John D. Mackenzie, Roddy Morrison,

John Macdonald (Carloway), Alistair Maciver, we put the world right as we passed the time for ourselves in withoning talk. And we had plenty of scope for talk in 1938 in the months leading up to the Munich crisis when Neville Chamberlain used a scrap of paper in lieu of a flag to semaphore 'Peace in our time' to a gaping world – a peace subsequently described derisively as 'the peace of God, because it passeth all understanding'.

I remember that one of the strongest critics of the 'appeasement' was John Macdonald (Carloway) – himself a disabled ex-service pensioner of the First World War. And when I said to him, 'I don't see why you should be so keen to start a war with Hitler. I would have thought that you would have had enough of fighting. After all, if it does start and things become critical, you could still be conscripted.' He replied with a chuckle and a slow grin, 'Oh no! I can't be called up. I was killed in the last war.'

With which remark, still smiling, and very much to my amazement, he took out his wallet, extracted a folded sheet of paper, and said, 'Officially I was killed in action, and just to prove it I always carry my own death certificate around with me.' Needless to say I was speechless.

Apparently while on patrol, I think that it was in the Salonika theatre of operations, he had taken a burst of machine-gun fire across the lower abdomen, had been left for dead, and was subsequently reported as killed in action. But, as I understand it, he had been found later by another unit, seen to be alive, and taken to a Greek hospital. Official certification of his death in action had, however, been received at his home in Carloway, and the traditional Hebridean wake for the dead was observed. It was some considerable time afterwards that his next of kin were advised that he was still alive although very severely wounded.

I could see that John got a lot of sardonic satisfaction from carrying that piece of paper in his wallet.

After the Munich crisis the discussions and arguments intensified, but although we still thought that we were putting the world right it went wrong in spite of us. We had our disagreements, but we never fought, and however emphatic our arguments they were always good-natured.

The supervising and managerial members of the staff were excluded by the very nature of their status from participation in the comradeship of the 'shop floor' discussions. That was their loss. As 1939 dragged on, on tiresome rubber-stamping feet, it became increasingly obvious that the Munich 'peace' had been a surrender, and preparations for a war that now seemed inevitable went on apace. We attended lectures on how best to protect ourselves against the ravages of mustard gas, and on other aspects of civil defence.

As the political situation deteriorated inexorably to the point of no return we received from Head Office code books on procedure. It was anticipated, quite wrongly as it turned out, that the bombing of our larger cities would commence with the outbreak of hostilities, and the first major civilian exercise was to be the evacuation of children to what were considered to be safer rural areas.

In this projected evacuation the Ministry of Labour was to be very largely involved, and those of us who had access to the code books knew that action would be instigated by a coded telegram from Head Office. The nature and the timing of the action would depend on the contents of the telegram.

One of the reception centres for evacuees was to be

Inverness, and, when the anticipated cryptic order to act did arrive, those of us who had chosen to move left that same night (it was Thursday, 31 August 1939) on the MacBrayne steamer *Lochness*.

The five of us who went were Donald Maclean, Ian Maclean, Colin F. Macdonald, Alistair Maciver and myself, and I think that just about the entire staff turned out on No. 1 pier to see us off and to wave encouragement. It was a truly beautiful Hebridean autumn night.

We were in Inverness by way of Kyle of Lochalsh on the morning of Friday 1 September before the Ministry of Labour office had opened, giving us time for a large and welcome breakfast.

When we did report we were immediately escorted to our 'digs', which had been booked for us in advance by the local management, and we were delighted to find that we were boarding together.

On reporting for duty to the reception centre on Saturday morning we discovered that the anticipated flood of evacuees was not even a trickle, and it looked very much as if there would be very little use for our services unless things speeded up later on.

On the morning of Sunday, 3 September, none of us could summon up any enthusiasm for the habitual after-breakfast walk. Instead we were hovering about the radio in the lounge, waiting for what we all knew would be shattering news, while at the same time trying to convince ourselves, rather hopelessly, that it would not be.

When, at eleven o'clock, the sombre announcement was made that we were once again at war with Germany, we five looked at one another in what I can only think of now as resignation.

Never again would things be the same for any of us.

SELECTED JOURNALISM

Discard the blinkers

Friday December 2, 1955

'What the eye does not see the heart does not grieve over' is an adage which puts into a nutshell a too frequent attitude of mind. But, though this proverb serves the purpose of pinpointing both human selfishness and the bliss of ignorance, it is regrettable that in many places and by many people it is acted upon as if it were a basic philosophic principle of life. And, unfortunately, the people who think in this way can often command sufficient support for their opinions to ensure that open, above-board, communal activities are proscribed and consequently driven underground; for, invariably, the result of proscription is not to eradicate the activities involved but to force them into secret session.

To my mind this is how the *bothan* originated – that canker that is eating at the heart of our rural life in some districts. The '*cèilidh* house' as it was known to older generations went out of existence and for a long time nothing was done to fill the vacuum. But man is essentially a social and a sociable animal and will not be thwarted in his instinctive desire to foregather with his fellows. The time was ripe and the way was open for a transformation of village life; but, instead of leading their people, especially the young, onwards and upwards as they could have done, the rustic fathers had nothing to offer. By that fact alone they forfeited the right to be considered as wise in their generation. But worse was to come.

The village hall system, with all the advantages which it could bring to country life, began to appear: and it is a poor comment on the sagacity and far-sightedness of allegedly wise men that in almost every district the village hall was opposed – on principle, moral principle, forsooth! By what perverted reasoning, by what affliction of intellectual astigmatism were these people able to see only all evil and no good coming out of a village hall? Did they not realise that by banning open social activities in their midst they were depriving their districts of the many benefits which could result, without obtaining any surety that the evils would be ostracised? Their only plea can be lack of fore-sight that they did not know what they were doing for they tried to veto the introduction of those centres and by that action forfeited the respect of anyone with even a rudimentary knowledge of sociology.

Unfortunately in some instances these kill-joys were successful with their veto; no village halls were erected; bigotry was in the ascendant; a 'moral' victory was won. The rustic fathers called the tune and now the youth are paying the piper as they go crawling in darkness to their 'bothans' to conduct themselves as they please, without supervision, while the elders who sent them there do not grieve in their hearts because their eyes do not see! What a furore they made when they opposed the halls and what a discreet silence do they now preserve! Would that the silence was born of a sense of guilt and that the sense of guilt might grow to such proportions as to harry them into trying to make amends.

I say in all soberness and seriousness, as my carefully considered opinion, that it would be a far better thing for all the districts concerned to have a village inn rather than one or two of these excrescences; that it would be infinitely more civilised for those who wish to do so to do their drinking publicly, within recognised hours and under supervision, rather than in the hole-in-corner manner of these dubious dives.

So you elder village-statesmen get organised! Get your feet on *talamh trocair* and get your heads out of the clouds! Stamp out these bothans even if you have to provide some alternative to help you do so. Go all out to provide all the counter-attractions to drinking that are available. Build your village halls and encourage music, drama, art exhibitions, instructional and other film-shows, debates, lectures, political discussions, 'Any Questions' sessions, concerts, dances – a whole range of unquestionably better things than 'bothan' or pub-crawling.

Or do you perhaps think that some of these things which I have mentioned are among the cardinal sins? If you do, just pause for a moment and consider that some of them are not: and consider that, if one accepts that some sins are more heinous than others, it would be desirable to eliminate the more at the expense of the less. It might even be salutary for you to wonder if you might be mistaken in your opposition to the gayer activities of youth: if it might not be a good thing to encourage them to foregather gracefully.

For thus the royal mandate ran,
When first the human race began:
The social, friendly, honest man,
whate'er he be,
'Tis he fulfils great Nature's plan,
And none but he.

Fighting spirit

Friday 9 December, 1955

Time and again I have noted that the Islesman invariably appears at his best in the face of adversity. When things are going smoothly he just lounges around and couldn't seem 'to care less': when things are bad he is up and doing, and the worse things become the more he ups and does.

This I have noticed particularly at sea: when the sun shines and the seas are calm he is inconspicuous; when the hurricane blows his capacity for action and his endurance appear to grow with the storm's intensity. This would seem to be a trait of Highland character – a trait which is probably responsible for the Highlander's reputation both as a seaman and as a fighter.

There is a story told of an old army colonel who met one of the former soldiers of his regiment and as they reminisced he said, 'Now tell me, did it ever occur to you, during either of the two wars in which we served together, that we mightn't win?' 'Well man, colonel,' replied the veteran, 'I never thought that we would be beaten – but there were two or three times when I thought we might all be killed before we won!'

Keep it simple

Friday 15 December, 1955

'See how from far upon the eastern road
The star-led wizards haste with odours sweet!'

In the more interesting and the more beautiful of the two languages which I am fortunate enough to speak with reasonable fluency there is a saying 'Nollaig an duine bhochd a h-uile h-oidhche a gheibh e i' – which is roughly translated, 'The poor man has his Christmas feast every night he can get it.'

That was said not because he feasted every night, but because feasts were so few and far between as to be remarkable; and in the times when the saying was born especially in these islands, the poor man's Christmas was simple to the point of austerity.

Not going further back than thirty-five years ago to my own early youth, to the days 'their heads just out of the mist of years long dead' when in the country villages of Lewis in the early post First World War years there was anything but a booming economy, very often Christmas morning excitement was focussed on one orange and one penny in the toe of a hand-knitted stocking. And when, earlier, I was still young enough to have a starry-eyed faith in the existence of a Father Christmas 'there was a war on' with the consequent restrictions on his largesse. Possibly that may be why there was so much simple pleasure in the orange – and the penny! – although by the time presents eventually did appear I was old enough to know that they came from a hand unpossessed of the saint's magical resources.

It is even possible that the joy derived from such gifts was greater than that of children who today have their nurseries filled with expensive toys.

I believe that children today also could get a greater and more lasting pleasure from simple things. I have seen a child on Christmas morning, surrounded by pounds' worth of toys and books, completely ignore them all and go into raptures over a scruffy little teddy bear, not more than nine inches high, clad in a small hand-knitted jersey and trousers. There was infinitely more joy for that child, not only that morning but for years afterwards, in her very ordinary little 'Cuddly' than in all her other gifts together.

Nowadays, unfortunately, children and elders alike are not permitted by high-pressure advertising to keep things on such an unsophisticated plane. Like many other worthwhile and worth preserving institutions, Christmas has been claimed by big business for its province and is commercialised ad nauseam.

With the backing of the large financial trusts the children of the poor can today celebrate the anniversary of their Saviour's birth on an extended credit basis.

There was a time when Santa Claus, as the personification of a business institution – if one can speak of a myth as personification – visited the homes of the rich rather than the poor, for Christmas as a business institution is no new thing – only the magnitude of the commercial ballyhoo is new. But in ultra modern times he can visit the poor as well; and what the rich pay in cash to preserve him as an institution the poor can now pay in instalments. And in a few weeks' time, in scores of thousands of homes throughout this country, broken toys will represent a percentage of unearned wages mortgaged to perpetuate what has become a money-making myth.

What was once an artless religious festival – and it is irrelevant whether originally it was Christian or pagan – has been boosted into a world-wide cash-raking racket based on the guileless faith of little children. And if there is one aspect of the sorry set-up that sticks in the throat it is that 'the faith of little children' should have become the foundation on which is based such a gigantic money-grubbing lie.

There are some things about the situation over which I become so indignant that my pen inclines to run away with me! So to prevent that happening I had better tell you that in spite of all the above I shall be observing Christmas like the rest of you. I shall be observing it because I believe in celebrating anyway – the man who cannot celebrate is already dead; and I believe in celebrating Christmas especially because of its emphasis on peace, goodwill, and selflessness: we cannot have too much of these.

But I hope that I shall be doing my share of it with more simplicity, and I hope more sincerity, than the garish advertisements and strident salesmanship of un-Christmassy commercialdom would have me do.

'Live and let live'

Friday 23 December, 1955

'One generation passeth away and another generation cometh: but the earth abideth forever', and although not so many generations ago, in rural Lewis, eagle-eyed snoopers sought with all their might to preserve the earth, they have now passed away, but the earth abides.

There are many of the older people today who remember what a sin against society it was considered in those times to cut a few square yards of turf on the common pasture; and any man seeking turf for the many uses to which it could be put on a croft went to cut it at his peril. How the rude forefathers of the Highland hamlets must stamp in their impatience through the fields of Tìr nan Og to see the land, a square yard of which they guarded so preciously, taken over in acre lots by squatters and plot-holders.

It was of course the first world war that started it on a big scale. The returned warriors, especially the younger sons who were landless and tired of 'roaming with a hungry heart', wanted nothing more than to settle down on their native heath; and that is what many of them did. They staked their claims in common ground and were not to be gainsaid by stay-at-homes: and although their activities were watched by jealous and resentful eyes in some instances, they felt that they had fought for their privileges and – what impressed those who would oppose them – they looked as if they were prepared to do a lot more fighting. Furthermore they had many ex-servicemen friends among the crofters too, for when you have fought side by side along with a man, whether on land or sea, whatever the traditional attitude dictates, the human tendency is to see things with the same eyes.

And so on the common pastures of almost all the townships of these islands the squatters established themselves, many of them doing really excellent work with the unpromising materials on which they started. Taking over land which had produced nothing since the peat was skinned from it but heather, moss and poor-quality grass, they dug it up, trenched it, worked it into productive agricultural units which are today in some cases producing far more than neighbouring crofts.

To see here and there two or three acres of once barren soil yield vegetables, potatoes, oats, barley, eggs and sometimes help towards providing milk, must be very gratifying to any landlord who has an interest in his estate. That is why the landlords have not only not vetoed the actions of squatters, but on occasion have tried to be as helpful as possible. The men who are producing two blades of grass where one grew before are making the estates on which they live better than they were. That is why, in my opinion, the landlords should not hesitate to give those of them who are doing well and asking for recognition some kind of status.

Accepting that the primary function of the Department of Agriculture is to increase agricultural production, it seems a strange anomaly that a crofter who lets his holding become rank and rush-grown from disuse should, if he wishes to improve his house on that croft, qualify for a loan, while a squatter or plot-holder who cultivates the ground in accordance with the best requirements of good husbandry, will not qualify. It should not be difficult for the landlords to judge whether a man who has been in occupation of a plot of ground for a number of years is a potentially good agricultural tenant, and, basing their findings on that judgment, give the necessary guarantees. And guarantees having been given, the Department of Agriculture could consider each case on its merits, instead of operating according to the arid wording of the act, however remotely the resulting action may be removed from agricultural production as such.

These proposals may seem revolutionary in some quarters, but no more so than the mere existence of the people on whose behalf the plea is being made would have appeared to our grandfathers.

'The old order changeth, yielding place to new' – and it changes because it is the pioneer in thoughts and deeds who alters the order of things. Among the squatters and plot-holders of these islands there are many of the pioneering type: men who made the barren soil fertile – and yet in law their children have not the right to inherit these plots of earth. Surely this right, among others, could be granted them.

'The genius raids, but the common people occupy and possess'. And the common people who occupied and possessed the barren land and made it fertile, who built houses and grew good crops by their own labours, who made oases where there were deserts, will leave the abiding earth the richer for their passing through it.

'A sweet disorder in the dress'

Friday 3 February, 1956

He had a reputation for being mean. But I never found him so. Possibly his reputation resulted from his disreputable appearance.

By the standards obtaining in the villages of rural Lewis in those days before the Harris Tweed trade boomed a new wealth throughout the island, he was considered very well off. Perhaps that is why he could dress as he pleased. Someone has remarked that only the millionaire and the tramp can dress without regard for appearances, the one because he can afford to, the other because he cannot. However that may be, my old friend's sartorial effects were always more picturesque than elegant and would have found favour with the most unconventional millionaire or tramp.

He invariably knocked on the door with his stick before he entered; and when he did enter his great bulk seemed to fill the small room.

The greetings over, he would draw his chair up to the peat-fire, light his pipe, clasp his hands over the crook of his staff, and then he was ready to launch on his evening's *seanachais*.

I found myself almost as fascinated by his appearance as I was by his tales; and in all the years that I knew him he always dressed in the same manner.

Homespun, fawn-coloured, baggy tweed trousers encased his legs and the legs of the trousers were rolled up to two or three inches above the tops of boots that had a little of everything that can be collected on Lewis crofts and moors clinging to them. The knees of the trousers had usually two patches apiece. These were all of differently coloured tweeds and little, if any, attempt had been made to match the main garment. The trousers were made with two seats to them, one of which was always worn in places so that the holes and thin transparency of the worn spots revealed the other.

From the waist upwards he was clothed in a rough grey working shirt, an ordinary worn worsted waistcoat, and, surmounting these, a fawn-coloured tweed jacket – but of course a different shade of fawn from the trousers. The elbows of the jacket were as heterogeneously patched as were his knees and from the bulging of his pockets one might think that he carried all his worldly goods on his person.

His tweed cap, to which straws and heather clung, was drawn well down over his forehead, above shaggy brows, twinkling kindly eyes, and a nicotine-stained beard.

The keynote of the whole ensemble was contrast, and there were so many patterns of tweed displayed that a designer might find much to inspire him in the sight.

Yet despite the unprepossessing effects of a first glance he was a most charming companion. His voice was soft and gentle; his fund of reminiscence and anecdote inexhaustible. He seemed, too, to remember every poem and song that he had ever heard and he often wove these into his stories, reciting in a pleasant voice or singing in a manner so modulated that the effect of age on his voice was scarcely observed.

Under the spell of his matchless storytelling, his reciting and singing, time lost all meaning and the longest winter's evening was all too short. And young though I was then, and late as he was persuaded to stay when he came, I was always permitted to hear him out, because no-one felt that I should be deprived of any of the magic of his presence.

He had been fortunate, in his young days, in being a boon companion of one the Island's bards. He was never tired of quoting his friend's words, or re-telling some of his stories, or singing some of his songs – as quoted, told or sung to him by their author over a dram in one of Stornoway's taverns. And a great many of these I had never heard before and have never heard since.

In that old head there was a fine book for anyone who could have gathered the material during the long winter nights round the peat-fire. It is a great pity and a great loss that there was no-one to do it.

He has been dead now for a great many years; and I at least, conscious of his inherent charm, shall always feel that a great many beautiful and precious things died with him.

More sinned against than sinning?

Friday 17 February, 1956

Gunpowder was discovered by the Chinese centuries before it was discovered in Europe; and it was used, as one would expect from such a highly civilised people, for giving fireworks displays at festivals and on holidays.

The people of Europe on the other hand, once they had discovered it, realised its power as a propellant, and in their own peculiarly bloody fashion, were soon using it for flinging lumps of iron at one another with unprecedented violence and satisfyingly murderous consequences.

While in Europe the Christian nations were improving and elaborating the capacity for the infliction of sudden death, bestowed upon them by the invention of gunpowder, the 'heathen Chinese' continued its use only to pander to his harmless taste for pyrotechnics. So it is not surprising to find that the Chinaman thought so disparagingly of the arts of war that he had a saying: 'Good iron is not made into nails, and good men are not made into soldiers.'

It is a far cry from the philosophy of old China to the reports of the Economic Research Council of Britain – but there is a slight if somewhat topsy-turvy connection between the two (an association-of-ideas connection

184

anyway). Old China only made soldiers of its bad men; and the Research Council declares that because Britain makes soldiers of her youth she makes bad boys of them before they become soldiers.

'The young people of today think of nothing but themselves. They have no reverence for parents or old age. They are impatient of all restraint. They talk as if they alone knew everything. As for the girls, they are forward, immodest and unwomanly in speech, behaviour and dress.' Now let me disillusion you right away – that is not a quotation from the Research Council's report. It was written, in fact, in the thirteenth century.

And in my young days when my own generation came in for a like criticism in like terms I always felt a glow of satisfaction in the knowledge that in the year 1274 exactly the same thing was happening for exactly the same reasons – and the same things were being said with just as much or as little truth. And the knowledge helped to confirm me in the opinion that although succeeding generations of teen-agers from the beginning of time have been declared decadent and the worst ever up to date – by their elders – they have in fact been no worse and no better than their predecessors.

I must admit that I thought that this was equally true of the present day. But apparently it is not. The young people today, if they are not worse, at least find a greater number of bad persons in their midst: and the Council produces imposing figures to prove it. In the past eight years crimes of assault and violence have doubled in the 17 years to 20 years age group. And if one goes back to pre-war days the contrast is even greater. In this same age group 163 persons were convicted of violent crimes in 1938: and in 1954, there were 762 convictions. An uncomfortable increase.

The Economic Research Council lays a strong share of the blame for this state of affairs on the system of compulsory military service; and it has no doubt but that the waiting for call-up is one of the unsettling factors. Now this is quite understandable; and anyone who has talked to boys waiting for call-up knows how demoralising the waiting process can be. On types that are already unstable the detrimental effect can be considerable. And demoralisation is contagious – others, both boys and girls, in the 'waiting' age-group are corrupted by contact.

This turning of youth towards criminal activities, this unsettling of the young, the removal of the sense of purpose from their lives just when they need it most seems to me too stiff a price to pay for the doubtful security conferred upon the country by conscripts. In the long run any military advantage accruing from the system may be more than offset by the evil which seems to be its inevitable by-product.

And in spite of the Research Council's figures one must remember that only a very tiny minority of bad hats is giving a bad name to a whole age group over a period of years.

For my own part I shall keep on remembering the thirteenth-century strictures on youth – and I would like to go on thinking that the young are, were and will be very much of a kind the world over. And if they are guided aright, in ten years time, the 17 years to 20 years age group will be very much the same as it was ten years ago – or ten centuries ago for that matter.

'All the earth and air
with thy voice is loud'

Friday 17 February, 1956

An axiom is a self-evident truth – if I may be forgiven for harking back to elementary mathematics!

And among philosophers it is generally accepted as axiomatic that certain basic values, such as truth and beauty for example, are universal. A development of this theme is contained in the saying that 'art knows no frontiers'. For art, in its different forms, is concerned with beauty and truth.

Unfortunately people who rule the destinies of lesser people are not so liberal in their ideas, and we find at different times, in different countries, a curtailment of the activities and the coming and going of artists which pays no heed to the ideal of universality.

Those of us who recognise that art, because of its very nature, cannot be bound to any country or people welcome any relaxation of artificial barriers temporarily erected by despots – whether the barrier takes the form of an iron or a nylon curtain.

That is why every lover of art, and of music particularly, must feel an upsurge of joy at the news that Paul Robeson has at last been granted an exit visa or passport, or whatever it is that a short-sighted US government department has been withholding from him since 1950, and that he is to visit this country again.

We, in these remote parts, who have to be content with recordings of his magnificent voice can only feel envy for and offer our congratulations to those people who will be fortunate enough to see and hear him in person. Someone once said that Robeson has a 'mulberry' voice, and to my mind that word comes closest to expressing its deep, rich splendour.

He is one of the finest male exponents of music through the human voice – which after all is music's finest medium.

I feel sure that many readers of the *Gazette* will join with me in expressing gratitude that the United States have seen fit at last to set free one of its outstanding citizens, and also to join in saying 'Welcome' to Mr Robeson when, on the occasion of his being permitted to move unrestrainedly into the free world, he makes Britain his first visiting place.

Paul Robeson does not belong to any country or people, to any class, creed or colour: he has a place above all these, a place in the hearts of men – men of all peoples and all countries, of all colours, classes and creeds.

'The Colonel's lady and Mrs O'Grady are sisters under the skin'

Unfortunately at the same time that a repentant (we hope) State Department was righting a wrong a most disgraceful incident was taking place in another part of the United States.

At the University of Alabama allegedly educated students in an allegedly Christian country were pelting a young lady with 'eggs, mud and stones'. The lady had committed no crime other than being born – although she had been most indiscreet in the choice of her parents and as a consequence came into this world with a differently coloured skin from that of the veneered hoodlums who stoned her.

When people have reached a level of education and erudition usually associated with university students one does not expect them to behave with the uncouthness and savagery of club-toting troglodytes guarding a cave. Their behaviour has been such as to lead free-thinking observers to the conclusion that the coloured lady to whose presence they raised such violent objections could only have bestowed dignity upon the campus – a lowering of its tone would appear impossible.

We are pleased to see that the President of the United States has 'deplored the rioting', and it is to be hoped that those in authority will read the riot act to the perpetrators of this crime against the human race.

Surely before God, after two thousand years of Christian civilization, it should be obvious even to a white American university student that the final application of human justice does not depend upon the colour of the human skin.

Moonstruck

Friday 13 April, 1956

Gaelic being my mother tongue, and having spent the first few years of my life in an almost wholly Gaelic-speaking school, it will be appreciated that when I was uprooted at the immature age of nine and transplanted to an almost wholly English-speaking school, my capacity for intelligent conversation with my fellows in the new language was rather limited. For a little time it was only after some cogitation and with the exercise of extreme care in my choice and enunciation of a strictly limited number of words that I could answer simple questions without conveying an impression of complete idiocy.

This was the unpromising material with which my long-suffering tutors were confronted; and, looking back, my sympathies shall always go out to the teacher who was responsible for directing my staggering footsteps on the path to knowledge and appreciation of English. And with my sympathy will also go the humble tribute of my acknowledgement that any subsequent capacity for understanding or facility in use of words followed upon an initiation given to me in a small country classroom; an initiation that could not have been bettered anywhere in the world. I know that it was there that the splendour of poetry first burst upon my mind; and the poem was

'Slowly, silently now the moon walks the night in her silver shoon'.

That moon then and ever since was mine as much as any man's; just as I knew that it was every man's as much as mine.

But, alas, it will not be so much longer. I see a headline in a daily paper which says, 'That's our bit of moon', and the article which follows opens with the saddening sentence, 'To which country does the moon belong?' which seems to me to confirm the truth that fools can ask questions that wise men cannot answer.

Just as the scientist turned the magic rainbow into the prismatic effect of raindrops upon light so it looks as if, aided and abetted by the 'embattled nations' they will ultimately turn the mystic moon into a bone of contention for colonists.

According to the Press, one of the organisations of the United Nations is to discuss the proprietorship of the moon and 'other legal conundrums of space travel' this year. It is suggested in a report to the International Civil Aviation Organisation that 'it will be necessary to make legal rulings for the staking of claims in outer space'. The report is also concerned with traffic problems and says that laws must be made to prevent man-made moons from jostling each other. And I suppose that with the laws will come traffic control – Belisha beacons among the stars, and inter-lunar zebra crossings! Will celestial traffic lights be erected? Will the merchants in lunacy transmute our civilisation into a radioactive if lifeless aura about our earth in a 'colonial war' fought over mineral rights on the moon?

Certainly there is a hint of moonstruck madness in talks of partitioning outer space or possessing the moon herself, and as 'luna' is the Latin for moon it could not be taken amiss if the first colonists were dubbed 'Lunatics'.

For my own part I would be much happier if she were left severely alone to 'peer this way and that' to see the 'silver fruit upon silver trees' or to watch the sleeping dog 'in his kennel like a log with paws of silver' – to do the many majestic things she has been doing since the first man breathed his first awe-struck line of poetry up to her sublime face.

I think that if ever the occasion arose I would find it necessary to register a conscientious objection to fighting either for a part of her or for the space approaching her. A clear sky and the opportunity to enjoy her from afar will see fulfilled all my ambitions about the moon.

Food for thought

Friday 20 April, 1956

Knowing the vagaries of human nature and especially the capriciousness of the human palate I have always maintained that if the common, and, in this country, much despised, herring were as scarce as trout or salmon it would not only be as much sought after, but would, as a consequence, demand just as high a price. Unfortunately, however, in spite of its excellent food value and the many palatable ways in which it can be prepared, and although there is a reasonably plentiful supply available in season, the ordinary consumer in this country treats it with disdain.

Now Trevelyan, in his *Social History*, has recorded how, over two hundred years ago in Scotland, 'the extraordinary abundance of salmon and trout afforded not only good sport, but a cheap food for the people', and he goes on to say that farm-hands went on strike if they were fed on salmon every day. Which would appear to confirm my opinion that as the supply increases the demand decreases.

Of course one can easily understand the attitude of the farm-hands who struck over a daily diet of salmon. And one can see that much the same would happen over too frequent feeds of herrings. But at the same time, as I see it, there should be scope for consuming a great quantity of herrings, or salmon, before the palate is cloyed and the consumer rebels. Provided, that is, that a taste for the particular food has been developed and maintained.

The taste for herring, instead of being fostered, is being allowed to die even in these islands, where it has flourished better than anywhere in Britain. Very few Islesmen of my generation would boggle at a meal of herrings two or three times a week. If this were true of the rest of the British Isles then the producers would have no marketing worries.

Tastes are mostly developed in one's youth – although they may be developed in later years as a deliberate act of will or necessity – and I fear that a great many children in Lewis today are becoming connoisseurs of macaroni and Spam, rather than of *spealltags* or *sgadan saillt*.

I heard of one youngster, who, one day during the school holidays, looked at his dinner in unfeigned disgust and said, 'Oh ghia, sgadan saillt! If I was in school today it would be Spam'

And there's the rub! Although the school canteen is an excellent institution and fulfils a too long-felt want, it is there that tastes are being formed today almost as much as in the home: and, with one or two honourable exceptions, no attempt is being made to provide traditional dishes or pander to the local palate.

Next month the summer fishing season begins, and the fishermen of the Minch will be trying to sell as much of their catches as they can in the home market as well as overseas. Surely the school canteens of Lewis could do so much to help out by putting on a lunch of herring, in one form or another, at least twice a week. Without hesitation I would say that by doing so they would be rendering a great service to the children by giving them a most nutritious meal and at the same time nursing their taste for herring, a service to the fishermen by offering an outlet for their produce, and a service to the local authority by dishing up inexpensive if excellent fare.

Granted this would conceivably mean much greater trouble than opening a tin of spam or ladling out helpings of macaroni and cheese. But it would be worth any extra labour that was involved.

In fact I see no reason why I should confine the suggestion to Lewis or Island school canteens at all. The whole of Ross-shire and Inverness-shire could pursue such a policy with advantage; and Nairn, Moray, Banff, Aberdeen and all the fishing counties of the North, in fact, could follow suit, operating on the principle that 'charity begins at home'.

Speeding up production

Friday 27 April, 1956

The world is now moving into the age of automation, and production is being so streamlined in some industries that a small percentage of the personnel at present required will be able in future to achieve maximum production. And although this will create a situation which will need considerable thought by all sides of industry that is not what I wish to deal with here.

Some time ago I came across a snippet of 'news' that is nearly a hundred and fifty years old which should, I am sure, prove most interesting to a people whose main industry is Harris Tweed.

In Yorkshire, which is also a tweed producing area, a gentleman by the name of Sir John Throckmorton wagered a sum of one thousand guineas that he would sit down to dinner in the evening wearing a suit of clothes that his sheep had been wearing as wool the same morning!

So, one morning, he had two sheep shorn; the wool was washed and dried, teased and carded, spun and woven. The cloth was then washed, dyed, and 'finished' while his tailor waited to start making the suit. The suit was made and Sir John was dressed for dinner at fifteen minutes past six in the evening. Shearing of the sheep had begun at five o'clock that morning. The year was 1811.

Not even automation could have much edge on that for speedy production; and I have often wondered if any of the local producers could equal it even with all the mechanisation of modern days. But I am not prepared to wager a thousand guineas on the result!

'True to the kindred points'

Friday 11 May, 1956

Summertime is here, and most people who earn their livings by keeping their noses to the grindstone for forty-nine or fifty weeks out of fifty-two have begun thinking about their holidays. Where to go and what to do? How to make the best of the all-too-short time at their disposal for rehabilitating tired bodies and minds? What would be to the best advantage of selves and families?

Thinking, or rather asking questions, along these lines and remembering last year's wonderful summer, I have come to the conclusion that there is a great deal to be said for staying at home; or at least for staying on the island if not literally at home.

There are beautiful, clean and easily accessible beaches and excellent bathing. There is fishing – loch, river and sea; moderately good tennis and bowls and very good golf. There is freedom from the eternal dash and hurry of almost all holiday resorts. And there are quiet country villages, where, from the point of view of reconstituting one's depleted energies, one can do nothing more constructively than anywhere in the world.

Just twenty years ago this summer I spent three weeks holidaying in one of those villages, and never before or since have I spent such a soul-satisfying time.

On arrival at my destination I discovered that a number of the villagers seemed to consider themselves my self-appointed hosts, and I was overwhelmed with invitations to visit their homes.

On the second day I had tea with one of them, and during a discussion that arose on the relative merits of education in Lewis schools at the end of last century and in the 'thirties of this century, my host – who had left school at the age of fourteen some forty years previously – astonished me by repeating extracts from Caesar's Gallic War and translating into English as he went along. He could have translated into Gaelic too! Then sitting round the peat-fire after tea he kept me spellbound with tales of the warlike exploits of his own ancestors with whose history he appeared to be as familiar as he was with Caesar's history in Gaul.

We chose the evenings for sea fishing: not being so much concerned with the fishing as with the restfulness of rolling easily on the surface of gently moving green water, but always making sure of fresh fish for breakfast the following morning. And extraordinarily fresh and wholesome it tasted, especially on the mornings when I summoned the energy to row round the bay before eating.

But what I remember most about the holiday is its utter restfulness. Many people maintain that the most restful thing that any man can do is to watch running water. And there is a great deal to be said for the claim.

My own choice, however, would be some cliff-top greensward on the Atlantic coast, a warm sun and a soft wind, with the air laden with the scents of innumerable flowers and herbs; to lie there watching the solan geese fishing; to see them poising against the sky, plunge like large white arrows into the blue-green sea, surface, and then the laborious take-off into the wind.

That, to me, is the most relaxing pastime that there is. So I think that it will be a Hebridean holiday this year for me and my family. And I have a feeling that at the end of it we will be much more recuperated than if we had been dashing by steamer, rail or plane for the much advertised and brochured attractions of the south.

There will also be the advantage, from my point of view, as a native, that we will have spent our holiday money in Lewis.

A place in the sun?

Friday 29 June, 1956

In Violet Jacob's poem the lad who is looking out of the window at the moon and who feels the call of the open road, says:

> When I'm as big as the tinkler-man
> That sings i' the loan a' day.
> I'll bide wi' him i' the tinkler-van
> Wi' a wee-bit pot an' a wee-bit pan;
> But I'll no tell Grannie my bonnie plan,
> For I dinna ken what she'll say.

But the days when there was any romance for a lad in the prospect of living in a van with a tinker-man are fast disappearing, and in this part of the world they have gone altogether. The 'old order' has changed and, unfortunately, the 'new' is, so far, shoddy by comparison.

I am one of those fortunate people who have the honour, because of beneficial experience, of being able to wear the same 'old school tie' – elementary school that is – as some of the tinkers. I have sat in class at school with them, played football with them, sat in their tents and talked with them; and even during the war found myself once, as a seaman, standing in the same pay-queue as a tinker whose surname started with the same letters as mine, and who, incidentally, wore on his naval uniform the campaign ribbons of the 1914–18 war in which he had served as a soldier. For these reasons I may perhaps be excused for embarking upon the controversial subject of the fate of these people.

Time was when the tinkers as we knew them were nomads – camped outside one village tonight and tomorrow night on the outskirts of another twenty miles away – pursuing their occupations as rag-collectors, tinsmiths and horse-dealers. But times have changed and waste-wool collecting has become the lucrative occupation of more 'respectable' citizens, tinsmithing has been made uneconomic by the marketing of machine-made, mass-produced articles of better quality and longer life, and horses have been ousted by motor vehicles and tractors. There are no longer any reasons extant for the tinker being a nomad and so we find settlements springing up in the place of temporary encampments. And, further, it is becoming increasingly obvious that some of these settlements are not altogether desirable and do not provide a way of life suited to recognised present-day requirements.

To my way of thinking this problem, and that it is a problem is clear, cannot just be ignored. The rest of us cannot go on with our own affairs, living our own lives, and conforming to accepted social precepts and, at the same time, treating these people as a separate society or as if they weren't there.

In this part of the world there is no colour bar – at least, not noticeably so. Coloured people are permitted to use our eating and drinking places, shops and all normal facilities without question; they are allowed to live among us without any attempt at segregation. The same treatment and courtesies are meted out to tinkers – until it comes to the point of letting them live among us. Then segregation creeps in – and there's the rub. A very serious rub it is too, for any right-thinking or free-thinking person, because the answer to the problem is not to put these people in a reservation, for obviously what were originally voluntary settlements are developing into reservations once those who are in them are prevented from leaving them. And on every occasion when some enterprising member of the tinker community attempts to buy his way out of his present environment and into ordinary society he is vetoed by authority.

Now history shows that the policy of keeping people on reservations leads to extinction. And there is no question but that an analysis of the present situation leads one to the conclusion that the fate of these people must be absorption or extinction. The only question that remains is whether we, as a society, are going to let them waste away or whether we are going to stretch out a helping hand in their struggle for adjustment to changed conditions. The number of them who are engaged on public works (some of their women even work in hospitals) shows that they themselves, have seen the writing on the wall as far as their former occupations are concerned. The fact that some of them are trying to buy houses and crofts shows a new awareness. They have done with the old ways of living. Are we going to hinder or help?

The time would seem to be ripe for a thorough and exhaustive examination of the position by the responsible authorities, a re-orientation of ideas about tinkers as a class, and the formulation of a progressive and benevolent policy to help them 'rise on stepping stones of their dead selves to better things'.

Deadline

Friday 6 July, 1956

One advantage of having to produce a written column of a specified length by a certain time on a certain day each week is that it must on occasion be good for my soul – in the same way as doing penance would be! Because whether a myriad of ideas are jostling each other for precedence at the front of my mind, or whether I feel as if my head had been filled with loosely-packed cotton wool, I still have to deliver the goods on schedule.

This week happens to be one of the stuffed-with-cotton-wool variety, and only the screech of a gull outside my window has stirred me into having a peep through the blinds to where full daylight is now spreading over a watery world.

As I sat and meditated – which is rather a flattering way of describing what I sit and do when my mind is more or less a blank – I had been remotely conscious that, beyond the curtain of studied, if unproductive concentration in which I had wrapped myself, a part of my brain which alone seemed to be functioning was registering the sounds of a faintly moaning wind and the patter of raindrops. So that my first glimpse of new day and a water-logged landscape, following the screech of the gull, did not altogether take me by surprise. What really does surprise me is that I am still sitting in the chair in which I sat down last night!

In my part of Stornoway, and I suppose more so in parts nearer the waterfront, the seagulls perform the same function of heralding the day as the cockerel does on the croft or the farm. But the crofter or farmer has the advantage of being aroused by the comparatively reasonable-sounding crowing of one or two cockerels while we have to suffer the strident screaming of a multitude of seagulls.

Of course at this time of the year it is often an advantage to be stirred bright and early; although of my own choice I would prefer a more musical method of announcing the dawn. My reason for considering an early call advantageous is that I think that in the summer time in this part of the world the best weather of the day is very often in the early morning; and I have frequently enjoyed several hours of beautiful sunshine before the late morning or mid-day clouds have gathered to blot out the sun and give us a dull afternoon.

It is just unfortunate that on this particular day, when I didn't even have to get up, as I am already, the weather sequence should not be working out for me. But perhaps instead of being unfortunate it is really the reverse in present circumstances. For if the sun was blazing outside my window I would find it extremely difficult to sit writing while the urge for a quick walk by the Creed or down by the harbour was dragging at my will power.

But today it is no punishment to spend the morning inside. Although the wind that was moaning in the night has died away, and although the rain has stopped, a dead grey sky still hangs low over the sodden earth, and the seagull that is strolling along the pavement outside my window, with the disdainful look that seagulls manage to achieve, is quite bedraggled; the jackdaw that is perched on one of the clothes poles in the back garden doesn't seem to have a 'jack' left in him – he even appears to have hunched himself up so that the rain won't run down under his collar. Only the cabbages in the vegetable patch seem to be greeting the day with delight!

Who knows? Perhaps today, things will work out differently and the leaden morning give way to a golden afternoon. And whether the day turns out fair or not the screaming gull that announced its advent is due a vote of thanks from me.

It gave me something to write about.

'Far away and o'er the moor'

Friday 13 July, 1956

The person in the song who sat by the light of the peat-fire flame and dreamed the dreams, must, if he had anything like my experience of arduous peat-winning, have been dreaming of something far removed from the *poll mònadh* and all its strenuous implications. And although it is all very fine to sit by a bright peat-fire, as I am doing at the moment, and to have the tangy smell of its burning in one's nostrils, I can never see peats either being consumed or being worked without remembering the back-breaking toil and soul-destroying thwartings that I suffered in my youth, cutting, lifting, re-lifting, barrowing to the road-way, and cart-filling the stuff, when I could have been much better employed, in my opinion, playing football!

In those days I didn't just work at our own peats, but at half the village peats as well, and from the time the first turfing started in April until the last cart-load was emptied and stacked in August or September, almost every spare moment, and some moments that I only spared with great reluctance, were devoted to one process or another in the accumulation of this frustrating fuel.

But at that time 'we were young, we were merry' and even if, to continue borrowing from Mary Coleridge, we weren't 'very, very wise', we were full enough of boisterous animal spirits to counterbalance the wearisomeness of uncongenial toil.

On one occasion I recollect cutting peats with a friend of mine on a day in early May, bitterly cold, with a north-west wind and frequent showers of hail. As we cut and spread the black, soggy slabs they were whitened by snow as we laid them down, while the handling of them on such a day abstracted the calories from our weather-beaten bodies at an alarming rate, and reduced our not very high morale to a bare subsistence level. Worse was to come, however, because when it became obvious that we couldn't stave off the pangs of hunger any longer we had to turn our attention to preparing a meal.

The fact that we were able to light a fire at all in the conditions that obtained would have earned us high commendation in any scout-troop! Fortunately my partner's mother, whose peats we were cutting, had no great faith in our capacity for cooking, and the sum total of our culinary endeavours consisted of heating up a dish of stew which she had already prepared, plus the boiling of some potatoes, without which a mid-day meal is not a meal in Lewis. But could we boil those potatoes? Through some oversight we had forgotten a lid for the pot, and as we crouched by the fire, we watched the hail-stones falling in myriads into the pan and, in melting, use up the heat that should have done the cooking. Finally, by mutual agreement, and spurred by the persistent gnawing at our vitals, we decided, quite arbitrarily, that they were 'done'. However, when it came to partaking of the Spartan repast 'underdone' would have been a gross over-statement of their condition. Yet as we ate this meal, vainly using every ingenuity to keep the snow out of our plates, and even out of the spoons (knives and forks being quite impracticable) on their journey between plates and lips, it was to a state of uproarious hilarity that our predicament moved us.

Then of course, at the other end of the season, there was the other extreme of climate calamity. Only a person who has suffered the tortures can appreciate what it is to walk from peat-bank to roadway with both hands occupied in holding on to a barrow while clouds of midges rise from the heather, and blanket themselves about one's head, with painful and penetrating persistence. I feel quite sure that many exiles from the isles who yearn for the white flame and the pungent smell of the peat-fire, spare little time for remembering all that goes into bringing that same peat from the *poll* to the *cagailt* or what they, themselves, suffered in the process.

And now I must tell you how I came to be sitting by a peat-fire tonight. A neighbour of mine borrowed my barrow to 'put in the peats' and when he returned it to me he did so in true, neighbourly and Hebridean fashion – full of peats!

All play and no work?

Friday 3 August, 1956

During my schooldays I was taught for a number of years by a teacher who on several occasions expressed his profound regret that it was necessary for man to work in order to live. His conception of man's status in the scheme of things was such that the development of the spiritual and cultural aspects of life was, for him, the only real point of existence. Fortunately this approach did not prevent him from making his pupils work, and work very hard too; but as his particular school subject dealt with the side of life towards which he was biased, he may have felt justified in achieving his ends by compelling us to toil.

Now my own attitude to work, stated in simple terms, is quite similar. I work in order that I may have leisure for all the pursuits outside working hours that make life worth living. And if I could achieve all that I am required to do in fewer hours of daily toil, and so increase the number of hours available for pleasure, I think I would not only be a happier, but ultimately, a better person for it.

The first results of the introduction of large-scale automation into industry both in this country and in America has been to instil fear into the minds of those engaged in the 'automation industries' that they will be deprived of the opportunity to earn their living at all. It is obvious to them that the same production can be attained by much fewer workers working the same number of hours as before. So naturally they come to the conclusion that fewer people will be employed in future and that consequently the unfortunate ones will end up on the scrap-heap.

But anything that can be done by one man working for eight hours can also be done by two men working for four hours. And I believe myself that when the more recent developments have worked themselves out and when all 'the tumult and the shouting dies', the result of automation will not be redundancy and unemployment but less working time and more leisure.

Not so very long ago the idea of an eight-hour day or a five-day week would have been dismissed as visionary by our ancestors who toiled for twelve and fourteen hours a day, six days a week, in order to live. Working, eating and sleeping occupied their time, and their leisure for cultural pursuits or play was virtually non-existent. To them a state of affairs which to us is now familiar would have been almost inconceivable and seem much more far-fetched than the idea of a six-hour or a four-hour day and a four-day working week appears to me at present. Nor is there any reason to my mind why these things should not come if increased production and the requirements of trade and commerce can be provided that way.

So press on with automation, I say, on the farm, in the factory and in the office; and press on also with the work of resolving the personnel problems involved. And I have no doubt but that when the loose ends are tidied up the result will be very much as I have visualised – less work and more play.

Up to the present, or at least until quite recently, the

ordinary man has not had the opportunity to become educated in the use of leisure; but in time that will be corrected, and given the opportunity he will be able to use his time as profitably for the improvement of his mind and of his person as do at present those who have had such facilities for many years.

Automation is another, and one of the greatest, strides towards the further emancipation of man. I only regret that my old teacher – who so railed against man's doom 'to live laborious days' – did not live to see it introduced, because I am quite sure that he would not have missed its implications.

Conviction and declaration

Friday 17 August, 1956

'They' had decided that we should have an identity-disc inspection. And 'they' were the term in which our much-harassed and discipline-dulled minds thought of all the directing power (from the petty officer through the various grades of braid to the Admiralty and Whitehall) that controlled our destiny. So an identity-disc inspection there was – each disc scrutinised; the name, number and religion called out in the peculiar dead-pan voice favoured by petty officers on such occasions, and used, I always suspected, so that the sound only and not the content was conveyed to the accompanying officer's brain.

It was all going fine – name, number, C of E, RC, and C of S, all good, safe religions – when it happened. 'Name, So and So; number, such and such, religion, MOS!' said the PO in a voice so startled out of its normal monotonous state that it even registered with the officer, who fixed the offending rating with an icy eye and said, very coldly and very clearly, 'And what religion, may I ask, is MOS?' 'Moslem, sir!' came the crisp reply. 'And how', continued the officer, who, if he had possessed a little more sense to eke out his lack of experience, would have left things as they were, 'and how do you happen to be a Moslem?'

'Well you see, sir,' said this personification of unorthodoxy, who had successfully brought the inspection to a standstill, 'when I joined the Navy and I was asked my religion I said I was an atheist. I was told, 'You cannot be an atheist in the British Navy. Must have a religion. Better think of one, quick!' So I said I was a Moslem, sir, and that was put down, and I've been a Moslem ever since, sir.' 'But why Moslem?' further queried the officer. 'It was the first religion I thought of,' came the answer.

But those of us in the ranks who knew our mess-mate, who knew that he had been born and brought up as an Irish Catholic before becoming an atheist, also knew full well that his agile mind had thought of many things before some rebellious devil deep down in his unorthodox Irish soul had made his tongue say 'Moslem'. And for my own part my heart warmed to him, because however much I might disapprove of his convictions I couldn't but admit his right to hold them, and admire his determination not to 'conform' even in the 'adoption' of a religion to be used 'for hostilities only'.

It was Voltaire who declared that however much he might disagree with a man, he would fight to the death to uphold that man's right to his opinions. It is a sentiment to which I have always subscribed; and I feel that tolerance is one of the greatest needs of society both nationally and internationally. The greater the degree of tolerance between man and man or between nation and nation, the smoother and more amicably will they work together.

Because of these convictions it was with mixed feelings of distress and disgust that I read of Renfrewshire Education Committee's decision not to give a teaching post to Mrs Violet Stein, and subsequently to turn down her appeal. She herself has committed no crime – but her husband is a Communist and is Scottish correspondent for the *Daily Worker*. So, as one member of the committee put it, Mrs Stein couldn't be trusted with the teaching of children in Renfrewshire. Now to me this is not only pernicious intolerance, but, even worse it subscribes to the dangerous doctrine of guilt by association – a doctrine which reminds me unpleasantly of the name of McCarthy, and earlier still, of an eminently undesirable character called Hitler.

Renfrewshire Education Committee should know that teachers can be and have been something much worse than the wife of a Communist. They should also know that injustice is injustice, tyranny is tyranny and prejudice is prejudice whether perpetrated by a committee of small-time big-shots or by the dictators of totalitarian states.

They should think again. When they are dealing with a confirmed Communist, or in this case with his wife, they know at least where they are: because after all, to draw a parallel with the preamble to this article, an atheist by conviction is preferable to a Moslem by declaration.

Peace at any price

Friday 24 August, 1956

The Fates, or whatever powers are responsible for making man commit a 'faux pas', must have sat nudging each other and rocking with hilarity when a BBC news reader told his listeners this week that Harris was in the south of Lewis!

Not since a vague Glasgowegian asked myself over twenty years ago if Lewis was 'somewhere in Skye' has anyone to my knowledge been guilty, because of ignorance of geography, of such lack of diplomacy.

These loose references to the territorial rights and claims of the Hearrachs are extremely dangerous and could precipitate a diplomatic crisis beside which the Suez situation pales into insignificance!

And what a time to choose for such haphazard comment! On the same day that the representatives of many nations are gathered together in the British capital endeavouring to preserve world peace, a misplaced word spoken thoughtlessly in a broadcasting studio strikes at the very foundations of good will. At the very time that the British monarch is 'showing the flag' to the natives and when the wild men of the west are forgetting their tribal rallying cries in their precipitate rush to prostrate themselves at the feet of royalty, at that psychological moment there goes vibrating through the ether a phrase that is almost an incitement to civil war!

Who knows to what depths of resentment and indignation the 'small dark men' of the southern hills are moved by such cavalier verbal treatment? At this very moment they may be preparing a fiery cross, or standing in groups by the newly-built peat stacks carefully honing their scythe-blades or corrans for a possible fray.

They know, these hardy sons of the rugged south, that their northern neighbour is worth watching. The Leòdhasach has always been land-hungry, and mayhap his appetite will be further roused when he is told that Harris is really part of Lewis. A thirst for power may stir his blood; and without counting the cost, or even computing the possible usefulness of acquiring a land of naked rocks, he may be even now girding himself for a war of aggression!

But we must insist that in spite of all incitements to action or counter-action peace must be preserved. Nothing must be done that can be interpreted as constituting a potential threat to the territorial rights of the Hearrachs. Nothing must be done by the Leòdhasachs that can be used by political instigators and agents provocateur to achieve their own nefarious ends.

Of course, many international observers (those who are able to view the situation dispassionately, anyway) have realised for a considerable time that the main trouble has always been that although Lewis and Harris are separated by a 'Gulf of Traditional Misunderstanding' they are separated geographically only by a small trickling stream.

It is also contended, by these same observers, that if the point of separation was more clearly defined it might be easier to preserve the peace.

Perhaps the real solution is to build a canal between

Lewis and Harris, joining the Atlantic to the Minch. The Harris District Council could ask Egypt to tackle the job; and with Egyptian capital, Russian technicians and native labour everything else should be comparatively easy!

Then the BBC could do its worst. Then North would be North and South would be South and never the twain would meet. And there would be no more stray sheep from Balallan or Arivruaich battening on the sparse hill-grazings of Harris.

Fact and fiction

Friday 7 September, 1956

'I can show it to you in black and white' is an expression often heard used to back up a point that is being questioned, or to give final convincing support to statements of alleged fact. However, after reading the daily press over the past month one is reluctantly led to the conclusion that if the 'black and white' is in a newspaper then, far from being accepted as the last word, it should be approached with the gravest and most inquiring suspicion.

At odd intervals in the past I had decided that with too many reporters 'a story', 'an angle', or just sheer sensationalism came first and that, in the pursuit of the exclusive, as in war, truth became the first casualty. Following the coverage given to the Royal tour of the Isles I sometimes wondered if the representatives of some of the newspapers concerned ever left their office stools; and I was more than ever confirmed in the opinion that, with some at least of those who did, straight reporting was the last consideration.

It is only when the full battery of journalistic publicity is concentrated upon one's own ground as it were, and upon things with which one is on terms of complete familiarity, that one realises what a tremendous deal of nonsense can be talked in the press and for what utterly inexcusable inaccuracies it can be responsible.

I am of the opinion that for most Hebrideans one of the results – not the least salutary – of the Royal visit will be a healthy questioning of 'what they see in the papers' in the future.

How much can be discounted of the reports of the African tour? When the Queen visited Ceylon how many of the 'stories' that appeared in the press can be taken as authentic and how many with a pinch of salt?

If a simple, straightforward, and highly organised business like a Royal visit cannot be re-hashed for us in print without all the dubious 'treatment', highly perverted 'angling', and mean sensationalism to which we have been subjected for some weeks now, then how on earth can we give credence to reports on matters that are much further afield and the truth about which it is often difficult to determine? How much can be believed of what we read about Cyprus? With what authority or authenticity does the press speak on Colonel Nasser and the Suez Canal situation? What are the facts and what the fictions about the 'war' that has been going on in Malaya for so many years?

Once the untruth, the inaccuracy, has been established, once the suspicion has been created, where does one draw the line?

A newspaper reporter for example, reporting in a now notorious case, said 'the men of the village (population 600), said . . .' and so on. On the morning that the item appeared in one of our dailies the population of the village concerned was exactly 137. A slight discrepancy is evident!

And the immediate reaction is to wonder in how many other cases are vital statistics more than quadrupled – or divided, by four, depending on which direction slip-shoddiness takes the reporter's footsteps.

Even if the public want sensationalism there is too much of it available already without the necessity of giving a twist to the truth. At present too many slick hacks devoid of literary merit are rendering a great, and what is worse, possibly lasting disservice to a great profession. It would be far better for those misfits to leave the field and to take up street sweeping or some other career for which their particular talents seem better suited.

Glossary

cagailt – hearth
corran, -ain – sickle(s)
Herrach -aich – Harrisman, people of Harris
Leòdhasach, -aich – Lewisman, -people of Lewis
Oh ghia! – expression of disgust
poll – bog
poll m'na(dh) – peat bank
seanachais – stories; storytelling
sgaddan saillte – salted herring
spealltags – (here, most likely) herring slit and fried or grilled
talamh trocair – terra firma; solid ground
Tìr nan Òg – The Land of Eternal Youth (in Celtic-mythology)